ETHNO ARCHITECTURE & INTERIORS
ETHNO ARCHITEKTUR & INTERIEURS
ETNO ARCHITECTUUR EN INTERIEURS
ETNO ARQUITECTURA E INTERIORES

ETHNO ARCHITECTURE & INTERIORS
ETHNO ARCHITEKTUR & INTERIEURS
ETNO ARCHITECTUUR EN INTERIEURS
ETNO ARQUITECTURA E INTERIORES

Aitana Lleonart

FKG

FKG

Editorial project:
2011 © LOFT Publications
Via Laietana, 32, 4º, Of. 92
08003 Barcelona, Spain
Tel.: +34 932 688 088
Fax: +34 932 687 073
loft@loftpublications.com
www.loftpublications.com

Created and distributed in cooperation
with Frechmann Kolón GmbH
www.frechmann.com

Editorial coordinator:
Simone K. Schleifer

Assistant to editorial coordination:
Aitana Lleonart Triquell

Editor:
Aitana Lleonart

Introduction text:
Marta Serrats

Art director:
Mireia Casanovas Soley

Design and layout coordination:
Claudia Martínez Alonso

Cover layout:
María Eugenia Castell Carballo

Layout:
Ignasi Gracia Blanco

Translations:
Cillero & de Motta

ISBN 978-84-9936-763-7 (GB)
ISBN 978-84-9936-761-3 (D)
ISBN 978-84-9936-764-4 (NL)
ISBN 978-84-9936-762-0 (E)

Printed in China

6 INTRODUCTION
12 LEMAIRE
18 SINGITA LEBOMBO
24 A BLUE RYAD
34 MAKALALI CAMPS
40 HOUSE IN IPORANGA
46 LAEM SOM
56 ONE & ONLY REETHI RAH
64 HOUSE IN IXTAPA-ZIHUATANEJO
74 AMAN-I-KHÁS
78 PORTMAN RESIDENCE
88 SYRIE-MANSOURYA
94 W RETREAT & SPA
104 RED ROOM
112 THE GARDENS OF SKOURA
116 GIRNAR
124 A PLACE IN THE SUN
132 VILLA DEL SETTECENTO A POSITANO
140 CAMP HOWIE HOUSE
152 PHINDA ZUKA LODGE
158 DIPLOMATIC RESIDENCE
168 ANDY WAHLOO
172 VERANA IN MEXICO
178 METHVEN HOUSE
184 LA XINA
192 BARBAROS BAY KEMPINSKI
202 WILTSHIRE HOUSE
210 NILAYA HERMITAGE
218 COMO SHAMBHALA ESTATE
232 PERFECT HOSTS
240 FOLEY AND CORINNA
246 DRAGON-I
254 ZEAVOLA SPA
264 GEOMÉTRICAS THERMAL SPA
272 RESIDENCE IN PASADENA
282 THE OBEROI VANYAVILÂS
286 ANGSANA MALDIVES IHURU
292 RIAD VERT
302 AMANPURI
308 DWARIKA'S HOTEL
316 HOUSE IN IBIZA
328 PURO HOTEL
334 RED CAPITAL CLUB
342 NOCTILUCA
356 BED
362 MAYA UBUD BALINESE VILLA
366 HOUSE IN HONDA
378 ASIA DE CUBA
384 RED CAPITAL RANCH
392 DAR LES CIGOGNES
400 MANDARIN ORIENTAL DHARA DHEVI
414 NOMADS
418 BAISHAYUAN TEA HOUSE
428 KAMATH HOUSE
434 VILLA SALINA
444 CHESTERFIELD
448 FUCHUN RESORT
460 EARTH SPA
466 BAMBOO GARDEN HOTEL
472 CHA JIAFU
476 TOUCH
484 CAFÉ SAMBAL
488 PORTOLA VALLEY HOUSE
496 CAMP HOWIE GARDEN
504 THE BLACK APARTMENT
514 SETTHASIRI PRACHACHUEN
524 LOTUS HOUSE
528 BAAN SANSIRI SUKHUMVIT
538 HUANG TING RESTAURANT IN THE PENINSULA PALACE HOTEL
542 GARDEN IN BERLIN-MARZAHN
546 ELENA STANIC APARTMENT

Economic and political changes in a number of countries in the Far East have opened up markets that have gained the attention of some of the world's leading companies. Japan is one of the wealthiest countries in the world; China's spectacular growth seems to have no end; Hong Kong is one of the most expensive cities on the planet; and India has become a coveted market.

In addition, as a counterbalance to centuries of Western domination, large Asian communities are to be found in the main cities of the Americas and Europe, preserving their cultures and disseminating them to Western socieities. Philosophies and religions like Zen and Buddhism bring with them all-encompassing values, such as harmony with nature and vital energy, which have found favor in the Western lifestyle. The spaces in which we move tend to place more and more emphasis on harmony in order to contribute to individual wellbeing and to mitigate daily stress. Ethnic inspiration has ceased to be a touch of the exotic and has become a tangible feature of daily life in our homes.

Distant cultures are the source of inspiration for this book, which explores the interior design of tranquil locations in Africa, Indonesia, China, Japan, and South America. The hybridization occurring in all these places is an ideal inspiration for those in pursuit of a captivating style. The contrasts between imperial and popular aspects of China, the explosion of color that is India, the restful contemplation of Zen, and the exuberance of nature in the tropics make the interiors and gardens featured in this book an endless source of inspiration for designing spaces with color, textures and imported furnishings.

The ethnic style is inspired by the warmth and tranquility that comes with the desire to live in natural and healthy settings. The choice of colors, the visual balance created by accessories, and a distinct selection of pieces from the most remote cultures lead to designs inspired by serene African lodges and Arab tents with their large cushions.

Ethnic decor conveys a fresh and tribal style, with saturated colors that are ideal for patios and exterior spaces. Crafted furnishings are a feature, particularly pieces made in teak, bamboo, and rattan, upholstered in natural fibers in neutral colors that are combined with geometric patterns inspired by African motifs and animal skins. In keeping with the same multicultural theme, auxiliary furniture is characterized by the delicate texture of wicker, cane blinds, raffia mats, handmade baskets, and pottery, such as ceramics representing totems or tribal masks.

Lighting features decorative elements like handmade brass or bronze Moroccan lanterns or lamps with plant fiber shades to enhance sensory delight. Leather lamps with wrought iron frames and patterns in henna and lamps with perforated metal shades are ideal for terraces and gardens. Candles are a wonderful accessory for lighting up the night, whether in combination with scents, incense or aromatic oil.

The pages of this book are a journey through the best projects that have succumbed to the charms of these hybrid aesthetics that are so exquisite and stunning. Readers will then be shown the keys to the styles of the most influential and traditional cultures, which will allow them to be reproduced as they are or with a more contemporary feel, always with the eternal enchantment of the ethnic style.

Die wirtschaftlichen und politischen Veränderungen in einigen Ländern des Fernen Ostens haben attraktive Märkte eröffnet, die das Interesse der wichtigsten Unternehmen der Welt geweckt haben. Japan ist eines der reichsten Länder der Erde, das Wirtschaftswachstum Chinas ist nicht aufzuhalten, Hongkong ist eine der teuersten Städte unseres Planeten und Indien hat sich zu einem sehr begehrten Markt entwickelt.

Als Gegengewicht zu Jahrhunderten westlicher Herrschaft sind große asiatische Gemeinschaften in den wichtigsten Städten Amerikas und des alten Kontinents präsent, wo sie ihre Kulturen lebendig halten und in der westlichen Gesellschaft bekannt machen. Philosophien und Religionen wie Zen und Buddhismus stehen für universelle Werte wie Harmonie mit der Natur und die Bedeutung der Lebensenergie, die auch im westlichen Lebensstil Einzug gehalten haben. Die Räume, in denen wir uns aufhalten, sind immer häufiger harmonisch gestaltet, um das Wohlbefinden zu steigern und den Alltagsstress zu reduzieren. Die Gestaltung im Ethno-Stil steht mittlerweile nicht mehr nur für einen exotischen Touch, sondern ist vielmehr ein Element des täglichen Lebens geworden.

Ferne Kulturen dienten als Inspiration für dieses Buch, das Interieurs herrlicher Orte in Afrika, Indonesien, China, Japan und Südamerika präsentiert. Die Vermischung der Völker aus all diesen Regionen bietet eine ideale Anregung für alle, die sich einen besonders attraktiven Wohnstil wünschen. Von den Gegensätzen des kaiserlichen und des volksrepublikanischen Chinas über die Achtsamkeit des Zen und die Fülle der tropischen Natur bis hin zu dem für Indien typischen Feuerwerk an Farben... die im vorliegenden Band vorgestellten Interieurs und Gärten stellen eine unerschöpfliche Inspirationsquelle dar, wenn es darum geht, Räume mit Farben, Texturen und Importmöbeln zu gestalten.

Der Ethno-Stil vermittelt Wärme und Ruhe mit dem Wunsch, in natürlichen Umgebungen zu leben. Die Wahl der Farben, das optische Gleichgewicht der verschiedenen Komponenten und eine sorgfältige Auswahl der Elemente aus fernen Kulturen tragen dazu bei, einzigartige Umgebungen zu schaffen, die von einladenden afrikanischen Lodges oder arabischen Nomadenzelten mit maurisch verzierten Kissen inspiriert sind.

Eine Dekoration im Ethno-Stil vermittelt Frische und ist aufgrund der kräftigen Farben ideal für die Gestaltung von Terrassen und Außenbereichen geeignet. Besondere Erwähnung verdienen die herrlichen kunsthandwerklich gefertigte Möbelstücke aus Teakholz, Bambus oder Rattan, deren Polster aus Naturfasern in sanften Tönen mit geometrischen Mustern im afrikanischen Stil kombiniert werden. Auch Kleinmöbel folgen der multikulturellen Linie, wie z. B. Accessoires mit Korbflechtereien, Bastvorhänge und teppiche oder handgemachte Töpfereiwaren, die Totems oder Stammesmasken darstellen.

Im Bereich Beleuchtung setzt man auf dekorative Elemente wie handgefertigte marokkanische Laternen aus Messing oder Bronze oder auf Lampenschirme aus Pflanzenfasern, die die Sinne bezaubern. Leuchten mit Lederschirmen, schmiedeeisernen Gestellen oder Zierelementen aus Weide sowie Lampen aus gestanztem Metall bieten sich für den Einsatz auf der Terrasse oder im Garten an. Kerzenleuchter mit Duftkerzen, Weihrauch oder anderem Räucherwerk sind eine hervorragende Ergänzung für die abendliche Beleuchtung.

Auf den Seiten dieses Buches entdeckt der Leser die beeindruckendsten Projekte, deren Gestalter dem besonderen und überwältigenden Charme der exotischen Ästhetik erlagen. Lernen Sie die Schlüsselelemente der einflussreichsten traditionellen Kulturen kennen, die Sie bei der Einrichtung eines Ambientes getreu übernehmen oder auf zeitgenössische Wohnumgebungen übertragen können und lassen Sie sich vom nie vergehenden Zauber des Ethno-Stils begeistern.

Les changements économiques et politiques survenus dans certains pays d'Extrême-Orient ont ouvert des marchés attractifs sur lesquels les principales entreprise du monde ont manifesté leur intérêt. Le Japon est l'un des pays les plus riches de la planète, la Chine ne s'arrête pas à sa croissance économique spectaculaire, Hong Kong est l'une des villes les plus chères du globe et l'Inde s'est convertie en un marché convoité.

Par ailleurs, venant compenser des siècles de domination occidentale, d'importantes communautés asiatiques sont présentes dans les principales villes d'Amérique et du vieux continent, conservant leurs cultures intactes et les transmettant aux sociétés occidentales. Philosophies et religions, comme le zen et le bouddhisme, apportent des valeurs universelles qui ont profondément pénétré le style de vie occidental, comme la symbiose avec la nature et l'énergie vitale. Les espaces dans lesquels nous nous déplaçons sont de plus en plus harmonieux pour contribuer au bien-être et atténuer le stress quotidien. L'inspiration ethnique a donc cessé de ne jouer qu'un simple rôle exotique pour se convertir en un élément palpable de la vie quotidienne, dans les maisons que nous habitons.

Les cultures lointaines sont la source d'inspiration de ce livre qui part à la découverte des espaces intérieurs de paisibles endroits d'Afrique, d'Indonésie, de Chine, de Japon et d'Amérique du Sud. Le métissage de tous ces territoires se convertit en l'inspiration idéale pour toutes celles et ceux qui recherchent un style envoûtant. Des contrastes de la Chine impériale et populaire à l'explosion de couleurs de l'Inde, en passant par la contemplation apaisante du zen et l'exubérance de la nature tropicale, les intérieurs et les jardins illustrés dans cet ouvrage constituent une source inépuisable d'inspiration à l'heure de donner vie aux espaces en y apportant couleurs, textures et mobilier d'importation.

Le style ethnique s'inspire de la chaleur et de la tranquillité, en harmonie avec le désir de vivre dans des milieux naturels et sains. Le choix de couleurs, l'équilibre visuel des compléments et la sélection remarquée de pièces provenant des cultures les plus reculées aideront le lecteur à créer des ambiances inspirées des paisibles *pavillons* africains ou des tentes arabes ornées d'immenses coussins maures.

La décoration ethnique transmet un style frais et tribal, avec des couleurs saturées qui la rendent idéale pour les terrasses et les espaces extérieurs. Elle est dominée par le mobilier artisanal, principalement en bois de teck, en bambou ou en rotin, avec une tapisserie de fibres naturelles aux tonalités écrues qui se marient aux dessins géométriques inspirés de motifs africains ou de peaux d'animaux. Dans la même ligne multiculturelle, le mobilier auxiliaire est caractérisé par la délicatesse de l'osier, par les rideaux de nattes, les tapis en raphia, les éléments de vannerie confectionnés par les mains d'un artisan ou les pièces de poterie, telles que les céramiques représentant des divinités totémiques ou des masques tribaux.

L'éclairage opte pour des éléments décoratifs tels que les lanternes marocaines en laiton ou en bronze, fabriquées à la main, ou les lampes aux abat-jour en fibres végétales pour renforcer le plaisir des sens. Les lampes en cuir à structures forgées et aux dessins au henné ou les lampes de platine trempée sont idéales pour les terrasses ou les jardins. Les chandeliers peuvent constituer une solution complémentaire pour l'éclairage nocturne, que ce soit avec des bougies parfumées ou de l'encens.

Les pages de ce livre partent à la découverte des meilleurs projets qui ont succombé aux charmes de ce métissage esthétique, si raffiné et étourdissant. Le lecteur y trouvera les clés des cultures les plus influentes et traditionnelles en vue de les reproduire de manière intacte ou de les traduire aux codes contemporains, sous l'envoûtement éternel du style ethnique.

De economische en politieke ontwikkelingen in sommige landen van het Verre Oosten hebben aantrekkelijke markten toegankelijk gemaakt waarop de belangrijkste bedrijven in de wereld hun blik hebben gericht. Japan is een van de rijkste landen ter wereld, China heeft een economische groei die niet lijkt te stoppen, Hongkong is een van de duurst steden op aarde en India is veranderd in een begeerde markt.

Daarnaast zijn er als compensatie van eeuwenlange westerse heerschappij grote Aziatische gemeenschappen gevestigd in de voornaamste steden van Amerika en het oude continent, die hun culturen intact houden en ze onder de westerse samenleving verbreiden. Denkwijzen en godsdiensten zoals de zen en het boeddhisme introduceren universele waarden die diep tot de westerse levensstijl zijn doorgedrongen, zoals de harmonie met de natuur en de levensenergie. De ruimten waarin we ons bewegen zijn geneigd steeds harmonischer te worden, aan het welzijn bij te dragen en de dagelijkse stress te doen afnemen. Zo is de etnische inspiratie niet langer iets exotisch en verandert in een tastbaar element van het dagelijkse leven, in de huizen waar we wonen.

Verre culturen zijn de inspiratiebron van dit boek dat interieurs van vreedzame plaatsen in Afrika, Indonesië, China, Japan en Zuid-Amerika onderzoekt. De mengeling van al deze gebieden wordt de ideale inspiratie voor iedereen die een fascinerende stijl zoekt. Vanaf de contrasten van het keizerlijke en het volkse China tot de kleurenexplosie van India, de bedaarde beschouwing van de zen en de weelde van de tropische natuur, de in dit boek opgenomen interieurs en tuinen vertegenwoordigen een onuitputtelijke bron van inspiratie bij het inrichten van ruimten met kleuren, texturen en geïmporteerde meubels.

De etnische stijl laat zich inspireren door de warmte en rust in overeenstemming met de wens om in natuurlijke, gezonde omgevingen te wonen. De kleurkeuze, het visuele evenwicht van de accessoires en een voortreffelijke selectie van meubelstukken afkomstig van de meest afgezonderde culturen helpen ambiances te creëren die zijn geïnspireerd op de vredige Afrikaanse *lodges* of de Arabische bedoeïnententen met grote Moorse kussens.

De etnische decoratie brengt een frisse, tribale stijl over met verzadigde kleuren, waardoor hij ideaal is voor terrassen en buitenruimtes. Opvallend is het ambachtelijk gemaakte meubilair, voornamelijk van teakhout, bamboe of rotan, met bekleding van natuurlijke vezels in ecru kleuren die worden gecombineerd met geometische dessins geïnspireerd op Afrikaanse motieven of dierenhuiden. In dezelfde multiculturele lijn worden de bijzetmeubels gekenmerkt door de verfijning van riet, door rietgordijnen, raffiakleden, de door ambachtslieden gemaakt mandwerk of aardewerk, zoals keramiek die totemgoden of tribale maskers voorstelt.

In de verlichting wordt gekozen voor sierelementen zoals met de hand gemaakte Marokkaanse messing lantaarntjes of lampen met kappen van plantaardige vezels om het genot van de zintuigen te versterken. Leren lampen met gietijzeren structuren en hennadessins of lampen van dun ajourgezaagd metaal zijn ideaal voor terrassen en tuinen. Kandelaars zijn een aanvullende optie om in het duister voor licht te zorgen en kunnen voorzien zijn van geparfumeerde kaarsen of wierook.

Op de navolgende bladzijden van dit boek worden de beste projecten laten zien die zijn bezweken voor de charmes van deze esthetische, zo geraffineerde en overweldigende mengeling. De lezer zal hierin de clous vinden van de invloedrijkste en traditioneelste culturen die hem in staat zullen stellen om deze ongeschonden te reproduceren of ze te vertalen in hedendaagse codes, onder de eeuwige betovering van de etnische stijl.

I cambiamenti economici e politici in alcuni paesi dell'Estremo Oriente hanno aperto l'accesso a interessanti mercati sui quali le principali aziende del mondo concentrano la propria attenzione. Il Giappone è uno dei paesi più ricchi del mondo, la Cina registra una crescita economica sbalorditiva, Hong Kong è una delle città più care del pianeta e l'India si è trasformata in un mercato decisamente ambito.

Parallelamente, controbilanciando secoli di dominazione occidentale, grandi comunità asiatiche impongono la propria presenza nelle principali città dell'America e del vecchio continente, preservando la propria cultura all'interno delle società occidentali. Filosofie e religioni come quella zen e il buddismo apportano valori universali che si sono integrati profondamente con lo stile di vita occidentale, come l'armonia con la natura e l'energia vitale. Gli spazi in cui ci muoviamo tendono a essere ogni volta più armonici per contribuire al benessere e contenere lo stress quotidiano. L'ispirazione etnica ha così abbandonato il ruolo di semplice sguardo esotico per trasformarsi in un elemento palpabile della vita di ogni giorno all'interno delle case in cui abitiamo.

Le culture lontane sono motivo di ispirazione in questo libro che esplora gli interni di tranquilli luoghi dell'Africa, dell'Indonesia, della Cina, del Giappone e del Sud America. La fusione tra tutti questi territori si converte nell'ispirazione ideale per chiunque sia alla ricerca di uno stile accattivante. Dai contrasti della Cina imperiale e popolare fino all'esplosione di colori dell'India, passando per la rilassata contemplazione dello zen e l'esuberanza della natura tropicale, gli interni e i giardini illustrati in questo volume rappresentano un'inesauribile fonte di ispirazione per caratterizzare gli spazi con colori, materiali e arredi di importazione.

Lo stile etnico si ispira al calore e alla tranquillità, in armonia con il desiderio di vivere in ambienti sani e naturali. La scelta dei colori, l'equilibrio visivo tra i vari elementi e un'accurata selezione dei pezzi provenienti dalle culture più lontane contribuiranno a creare ambienti ispirati ai tranquilli *lodge* africani o alle tipiche tende arabe con grandi cuscini moreschi.

L'arredamento etnico trasmette uno stile fresco e tribale con colori saturi, la scelta ideale per terrazze e spazi esterni. Si impongono i mobili di fattura artigianale, principalmente in legno di teak, bambù o rattan, con tappezzerie in fibre naturali dai toni grezzi, combinati a disegni geometrici che si ispirano a motivi africani o alle pelli degli animali. Seguendo lo stesso approccio multiculturale, gli arredi aggiuntivi si caratterizzano per la delicatezza del vimini, per le tende di paglia o i pezzi di terracotta come le ceramiche che rappresentano divinità totemiche o maschere tribali.

Nell'illuminazione si opta per elementi decorativi come le tipiche lanterne marocchine di ottone o bronzo, realizzate a mano, o le lampade con paralume in fibra vegetale per potenziare il piacere dei sensi. Le lampade di cuoio con strutture in ferro battuto e disegni di hennè o quelle in metallo sono ideali per terrazze o giardini. I candelabri saranno un'opzione aggiuntiva per illuminare le serate con candele profumate o incensi di vario tipo.

Le pagine di questo libro propongono un percorso attraverso i migliori progetti che hanno ceduto al fascino di questa fusione estetica, così sofisticata e coinvolgente. Il lettore troverà nelle pagine seguenti le chiavi delle culture più influenti e tradizionali che gli consentiranno di riprodurle integralmente o coniugarle secondo i codici contemporanei, sotto l'eterna fascinazione dello stile etnico.

Los cambios económicos y políticos en algunos países del Lejano Oriente han abierto atractivos mercados en los que las principales empresas del mundo tienen puestas sus miradas. Japón es uno de los países más ricos del mundo, el crecimiento económico de China es imparable, Hong Kong es una de las ciudades más caras del planeta y la India se ha transformado en un codiciado mercado.

Asimismo, como contrapartida a siglos de dominación occidental, grandes comunidades asiáticas están presentes en las principales ciudades de América y del viejo continente, manteniendo intactas sus culturas y difundiéndolas en las sociedades occidentales. Filosofías y religiones como el zen y el budismo aportan unos valores universales que han calado profundamente en el estilo de vida occidental, como la armonía con la naturaleza y la energía vital. Los espacios en los que nos movemos tienden a ser cada vez más armónicos para contribuir al bienestar y mitigar el estrés diario. Así pues, la inspiración étnica ha dejado de ser una mirada exótica para convertirse en un elemento palpable de la vida diaria, en las casas que habitamos.

Las culturas lejanas son el motivo de inspiración en este libro que explora los interiores de plácidos lugares de África, Indonesia, China, Japón y América del Sur. El mestizaje de todos estos territorios se convierte en la inspiración ideal para todo aquel que busca un estilo cautivador. Desde los contrastes de la China imperial y popular, hasta la explosión de color de la India, pasando por la contemplación reposada del zen y la exhuberancia de la naturaleza tropical, los interiores y jardines contenidos en este volumen representan una inagotable fuente de inspiración a la hora de ambientar los espacios con colores, texturas y mobiliario de importación.

El estilo étnico se inspira en la calidez y la tranquilidad acordes con el deseo de vivir en ambientes naturales y sanos. La elección de colores, el equilibrio visual de los complementos y una distinguida selección de piezas provinentes de las culturas más recónditas ayudarán a crear espacios inspirados en los plácidos *lodges* africanos o en las jaimas árabes con amplios cojines morunos.

La decoración étnica transmite un estilo fresco, tribal y lleno de colorido, lo que resulta ideal para terrazas y espacios exteriores. Destaca el mobiliario artesanal, principalmente de madera de teca, bambú o ratán, con tapicería de fibras naturales de tonalidades crudas que se combinan con dibujos geométricos inspirados en motivos africanos o pieles de animales. Siguiendo la misma línea multicultural, el mobiliario auxiliar se caracteriza por la delicadeza del mimbre, las cortinas de estera, las alfombras de rafia, los elementos de cestería trabajados por las manos de un artesano o las piezas de alfarería, tales como cerámicas que representan a dioses totémicos o máscaras tribales.

En la iluminación se opta por elementos decorativos como faroles marroquíes de latón o bronce, hechos a mano, o lámparas con pantallas de fibras vegetales para potenciar el placer de los sentidos. Las lámparas de piel con estructuras de forja y dibujos de alheña o las lámparas de pletina calada son ideales para terrazas o jardines. Los candelabros serán una opción complementaria para iluminar las noches, ya sea con velas perfumadas, inciensos o sahumerios.

Las páginas de este libro proponen un recorrido por los mejores proyectos que han sucumbido a los encantos de este mestizaje estético, tan exquisito y abrumador. A continuación el lector encontrará las claves de las más influyentes y tradicionales culturas que le permitirán reproducirlas intactas o traducirlas a los códigos contemporáneos, bajo el eterno hechizo del estilo étnico.

LEMAIRE

Jérôme Le Maire, Sylvia Sepulchre // www.douar-tajanate.com // © Jean-Pierre Gabriel

This interior uses warmth to reinterpret tradition, with rooms that combine rustic restored elements, which preserve the beauty of the old, with other details like raffia rugs under the bed or baskets strategically positioned in a corner of the bedroom. In the garden, large cushions have been arranged beneath the arches of the porch, which constitutes the perfect place for drinking tea.

Cet intérieur réinterprète l'aspect chaleureux de la tradition, avec des objets qui mêlent les éléments rustiques restaurés, préservant ainsi la beauté de l'ancien, à d'autres détails, à l'instar des tapis de raphia sous le lit ou des paniers sciemment placés dans un coin de la pièce. Dans le jardin, de grands coussins sont disposés sous les arcades du porche, devenant ainsi un espace idéal pour prendre le thé.

Questo interno reinterpreta la tradizione per creare uno spazio accogliente, con ambienti che fondono elementi rustici, restaurati allo scopo di preservare la bellezza dell'antico, con altri dettagli, quali tappeti di rafia sotto ai letti o ceste strategicamente disposte negli angoli delle camere. In giardino, grandi cuscini sono stati sistemati sotto gli archi del portico, che costituisce il luogo ideale dove prendere un tè.

Dieses Interieur versteht Bautradition unter dem Aspekt Wärme. Die Zimmer enthalten eine Mischung aus restaurierten rustikalen Objekten, deren Schönheit erhalten werden soll, und anderen Details wie den Bastteppichen unter dem Bett oder den Körben, die strategisch in einer Ecke des Zimmers aufgestellt wurden. Im Garten, unterhalb der Bögen der Veranda, liegen Kissen, ein idealer Platz für die Teestunde.

In dit interieur wordt de traditie opnieuw geïnterpreteerd met warmte als uitgangspunt. In de ruimtes worden landelijke, gerestaureerde elementen gecombineerd om de schoonheid van het oude te behouden, naast andere details zoals raffia kleden onder het bed of strategisch geplaatste manden in een hoek van de kamer. In de tuin zijn onder de bogen van de veranda enkele grote kussens neergelegd.

Este interior reinterpreta la tradición desde la calidez, con estancias que mezclan elementos rústicos, restaurados para preservar la belleza de lo antiguo, con otros detalles, como alfombras de rafia bajo la cama o cestos colocados estratégicamente en un rincón de la habitación. En el jardín, unos grandes cojines han sido dispuestos bajo las arcadas del porche para ofrecer un espacio ideal para tomar el té.

SINGITA LEBOMBO

Cécile and Boyd's Interior Design // www.cecileandboyds.co.za // © Singita Lebombo

The hotel is a refuge in the wild where guests can enjoy the typical local architecture of thick adobe walls and straw roofs. It is possible to stay in a variety of bungalows with views over the river, decorated with wood carvings and equipped with colonial style canopy beds.

Das Hotel wird zu einem Schutzort in der Wildnis, die Gäste können die für die Region typische Bauweise mit dicken Lehmmauern und Strohdächern fühlen. Mit Blick auf den Fluss kann man in verschiedensten Bungalows logieren, die mit geschnitzten Holzmöbeln und mit Himmelbetten im Kolonialstil ausgestattet sind.

L'hôtel se transforme en refuge sauvage où les hôtes bénéficient d'une architecture typique de la région, aux murs rustiques en pisé et toits de paille. Pour se loger, les hôtes ont le choix entre divers bungalows avec vue sur le fleuve, décorés de bois sculptés et de lits à baldaquin de style colonial.

Het hotel verandert in een toevluchtsoord in de wildernis, waar de gasten kunnen genieten van een voor de streek kenmerkende architectuur, met dikke adobe muren en rieten daken. Het is mogelijk om te verblijven in een van de bungalows met uitzicht op de rivier, ingericht met houtsnijwerk en voorzien van bedden met baldakijnen in koloniale stijl.

L'hotel è un rifugio selvaggio dove gli ospiti possono godere dell'architettura tipica della zona, caratterizzata da pareti spesse di adobe e tetti di paglia. È possibile alloggiare in diversi bungalow con vista al fiume, adornati con oggetti di legno intagliato e con letti a baldacchino in stile coloniale.

El hotel se convierte en un refugio salvaje donde los huéspedes pueden disfrutar de una arquitectura típica de la zona, con paredes gruesas de adobe y techos de paja. Es posible alojarse en una variedad de bungalows con vistas al río, decorados con piezas de madera tallada y dotados de camas con dosel de estilo colonial.

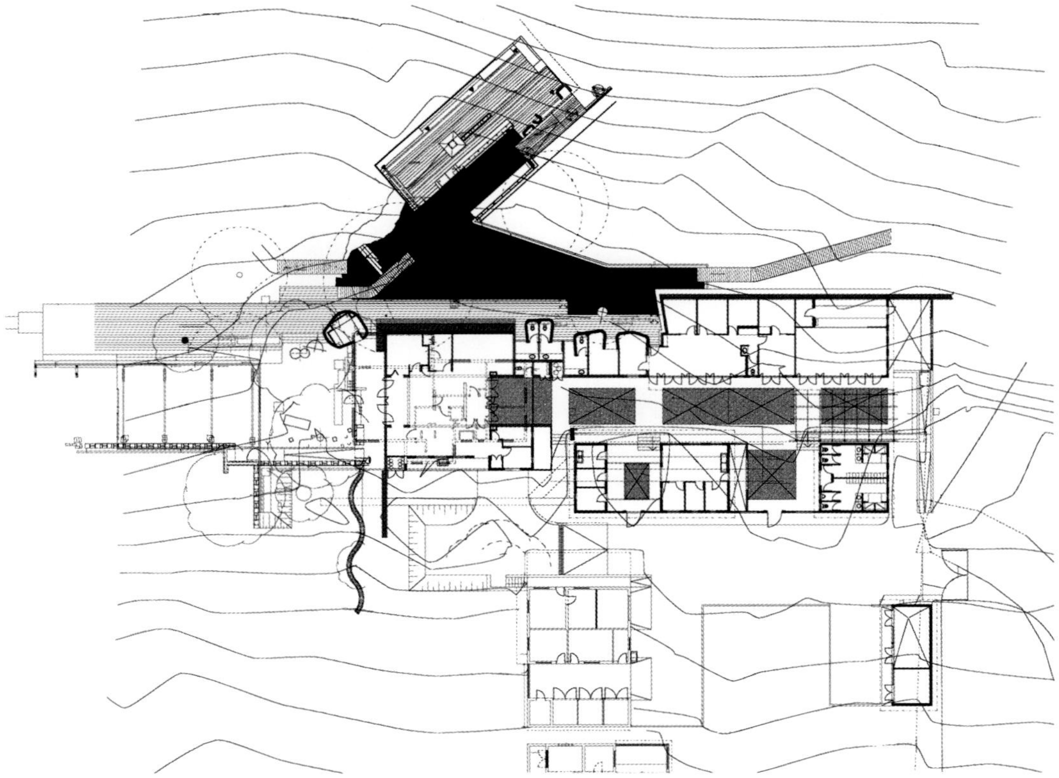

Ground floor

A BLUE RYAD

Emery & Cie/Agnès Emery // www.emeryetcie.com // © L. Wauman/Inside/Cover

The Moroccan mosaic stands out that covers the floor and part of the walls, which are finished in an intense blue, contrasting with the white ceiling. The interior follows traditional decoration, with wooden and iron furniture, Arabian cloths and the Moroccan trademark of mosaics that run through the rooms.

On y remarque la mosaïque marocaine qui couvre le sol et une partie des murs et colonnes, d'un bleu intense qui contraste avec le bleu de la toiture. L'intérieur reflète la décoration traditionnelle, avec meubles en bois et fer forgé, tentures arabes et le perpétuel sceau marocain des mosaïques qui parcourent les pièces.

Al piano terra, nel cortile chiuso da archi, tipico dell'architettura islamica, è da notare il mosaico che copre il pavimento e parte delle pareti e delle colonne, coronate da un blu intenso che fa da contrasto al bianco della copertura. Gli interni seguono la decorazione tradizionale, con mobili di legno e ferro battuto, tele arabe e il consueto marchio marocchino dei mosaici, che abbelliscono gli ambienti.

Auffallend sind die marokkanischen Mosaiksteine der Böden und an Teilen der Wände und Säulen, mit Abschlusskanten in kräftigem Blau, welches einen Kontrast zur weißen Farbe der Decke bildet. Der Innenraum wurde nach traditioneller Weise dekoriert, mit Möbeln aus Holz und Schmiedeeisen, arabischen Stoffmustern und Mosaikböden in allen Räumen, das zeitlose Markenzeichen Marokkos.

Opvallend is het Marokkaanse mozaïek waarmee de vloer en een deel van de wanden en zuilen bedekt is, afgewerkt in intens blauw dat contrasteert met het wit van het dak. Binnen is de traditionele inrichting voortgezet, met houten en gesmede meubels, Arabische doeken en de onvergankelijke Marokkaanse stempel van de mozaïeken die in alle vertrekken terugkomt.

Destaca el mosaico marroquí que cubre el suelo y parte de las paredes y columnas, rematadas con un azul intenso que contrasta con el blanco de la cubierta. El interior sigue la decoración tradicional, con muebles de madera y forja, telas árabes y el perenne sello marroquí de los mosaicos que recorren las estancias.

MAKALALI CAMPS

Silvio Rech, Lesley Carstens, Architecture & Interior Architecture // adventarch@mweb.co.za // © S. Dos Santos/Inside/Cover

Hidden among the vegetation is this lodge located on a South African reserve, characterized by the wooden construction and straw roof of its bungalows, which provide a refreshing and comfortable space for guests. The bedrooms are equipped with canopy beds and bathrooms where the African details, like masks or ethnic mosaics, stand out.

Masqué par la végétation, ce lodge situé dans une réserve sud africaine se définit par la construction en bois et la toiture de paille de ses bungalows qui offrent à ses hôtes un espace frais et confortable. Dans les chambres, dotées de lit à baldaquin et de salles de bain, les détails africains sont à l'honneur, à l'instar des masques et mosaïques ethniques.

Nascosto in mezzo alla vegetazione, questo lodge situato in una riserva naturale sudafricana è caratterizzato dalla struttura di legno con copertura di paglia dei bungalow, dove i clienti possono godere di uno spazio fresco e accogliente. Le camere sono provviste di letti a baldacchino e bagni, nei quali sono notevoli i dettagli africani, come le maschere e i mosaici in stile etnico.

Diese Lodge, versteckt in der Vegetation eines Naturreservats in Südafrika, zeichnet sich durch die Konstruktionsweise seiner Bungalows aus Holz und Strohdächern aus, welche den Gästen eine kühle und bequeme Unterkunft bieten. Die Zimmer sind mit Himmelbetten und privatem Bad ausgestattet, in den Badezimmern stechen die afrikanischen Objekte wie ethnische Masken und Mosaike ins Auge.

Deze tussen de begroeiing verborgen *lodge*, gelegen in een Zuid-Afrikaanse reserve, wordt gekenmerkt door de houten structuur met een rieten dak van de bungalows. De kamers hebben bedden met baldakijnen en badkamers waarin Afrikaanse details, zoals maskers en etnische mozaïeken opvallen.

Oculto entre la vegetación, este *lodge* situado en una reserva sudafricana se caracteriza por la estructura de madera con cubierta de paja de sus bungalows. Las habitaciones están provistas de camas con dosel y baños en los que destacan los detalles africanos, como máscaras y mosaicos étnicos.

AFRICA

HOUSE IN **IPORANGA**

Arthur Casas Arquitetura e Design // www.arthurcasas.com.br // © Tuca Reinés

Located in the middle of a forest, in a peaceful and serene setting that is ideal for recharging your batteries, this house had to be an extension of its surroundings. It is a comfortable home, a reflection of the owner's interests. On display in the studio are ethnic pieces bought on different trips.

Située au coeur d'un bois, dans un environnement calme et agréable où puiser de l'énergie nouvelle, cette maison s'affiche volontairement en prolongement de la sérénité du paysage environnant. C'est un habitat confortable, reflet des préoccupations du propriétaire. Le studio expose quelques objets ethniques achetés au gré de différents voyages.

Situata in mezzo a un bosco, in un ambiente tranquillo e gradevole dove è possibile recuperare le proprie forze, questa casa è stata pensata come un'estensione della pace che la circonda. È un spazio accogliente che riflette le inquietudini del proprietario. Alcuni oggetti in stile etnico, acquistati nel corso di diversi viaggi, sono esposti nello studio.

Mitten in einem Waldstück gelegen, in einer friedlichen und ruhigen Lage, in der man neue Energien tanken kann, ist dieses Haus eine sinnvolle Ergänzung zu seiner Umgebung. Es handelt sich um einen komfortablen Wohnraum, der den Interessen des Eigentümers entspricht. Im Arbeitszimmer sind einige ethnische Objekte ausgestellt, die auf verschiedenen Reisen erworben wurden.

Dit huis, gelegen midden in het bos, in een rustige en aangename omgeving, waar men op adem kan komen, moest een verruiming van de rust van de omgeving worden. Het is een comfortabele woning, waarin de aspiraties van de eigenaar worden weerspiegeld. In de werkruimte worden enkele etnische kunstwerken tentoongesteld die tijdens verschillende reizen zijn aangeschaft.

Situada en medio de un bosque, en un entorno sosegado y agradable donde es posible reponer energías, esta casa debía ser una extensión de la tranquilidad de los alrededores. Se trata de un hábitat confortable, reflejo de las inquietudes del propietario. En el estudio se exponen algunas piezas étnicas compradas en diferentes viajes.

indiamodern
PHAIDON

RM SCHINDLER

LAEM SOM

Jean-Michel Gathy/Denniston Internacional Architects // www.denniston.com.my // © Marc Barbay

The buildings feature elements of traditional Thai architecture such as the roofs, with the beams becoming a focal point of the interior design. The majority of the materials have been used in their natural state, such as the granite stones of the retaining walls or the native Thai teak.

Les constructions comportent des éléments de l'architecture traditionnelle thaïlandaise, comme par exemple les toits, dont les supports deviennent un élément central de la décoration. Une grande partie des matériaux ont été utilisés dans leur état naturel, comme les pierres de granite composant les murs de soutènement, ou encore le bois de teck provenant des arbres autochtones de Thaïlande.

Gli edifici presentano aspetti dell'architettura tradizionale tailandese come i tetti, i cui supporti si trasformano in un elemento centrale degli arredi. La maggior parte dei materiali è stata utilizzata allo stato naturale, come le pietre in granito dei muri di contenimento o il legno di teak proveniente da alberi autoctoni tailandesi.

Die Gebäude enthalten Bauteile traditioneller thailändischer Architektur wie z. B. die Dächer, deren Träger zu einem zentralen Zierelement werden. Ein Großteil der Baumaterialien, wie die Granitsteine der Stützmauern und das Teakholz von bodenständigen Bäumen aus Thailand, wurde naturbelassen eingesetzt.

De gebouwen hebben elementen uit de traditionele Thaise architectuur, zoals de daken waarvan de dragers zijn uitgegroeid tot een centraal element in de inrichting. Een groot deel van de materialen is in natuurlijke staat gebruikt, zoals de granietsteen van de steunmuren of het teakhout, afkomstig van autochtone bomen van Thailand.

Las edificaciones contienen elementos de la arquitectura tradicional tailandesa, como las cubiertas, cuyos soportes se han convertido en un elemento central de la decoración. Gran parte de los materiales han sido utilizados en su estado natural, como las piedras de granito de los muros de contención o la madera de teca proveniente de árboles autóctonos de Tailandia.

Japan

ONE & ONLY REETHI RAH

ESPA International // www.espaonline.com // © Barbara Kraft

The Reethi Rah resort's spa blends the Oriental with the local. It was designed by ESPA, the world's foremost spa consultant. Built with stone walls and straw roofs, the traditional style of the eight villas in the spa complex is meant to maintain a harmonious nexus with nature.

Le complexe hôtelier Reethi Rah abrite un spa, conçu par l'entreprise spécialisée ESPA, qui conjugue caractère local et caractère oriental. Bâties avec des murs en pierre et des toits en paille, les huit villas du pavillon du spa sont décorées selon une esthétique faisant appel au style traditionnel en vue de conserver un lien harmonieux avec l'environnement.

Il resort Reethi Rah ospita una spa che combina tradizione locale e orientale, progettata dalla società specializzata ESPA. Realizzate con pareti in pietra e tetti di paglia, le otto ville del padiglione del centro benessere sono state progettate seguendo un'estetica che richiama lo stile tradizionale, per un'armoniosa integrazione nel contesto circostante.

Das Resort Reethi Rah beherbergt ein vom Unternehmen ESPA entworfenes Spa, das lokale Elemente mit orientalischen Akzenten kombiniert. Die acht Pavillons mit Steinwänden und Strohdächern wurden im traditionellen Stil gehalten, um eine harmonische Verbindung mit der Umgebung zu erzielen.

Het Reethi Rah resort heeft een spa waarin plaatselijke elementen met oriëntaalse worden gecombineerd. Het concept is bedacht door de gespecialiseerde firma ESPA. Het resort is gebouwd met stenen muren en rieten daken en de acht villa's van het paviljoen van de spa zijn ontworpen volgens een esthetiek die de traditionele stijl aanhoudt als manier om een harmonieuze verbinding met de omgeving te behouden.

El *resort* Reethi Rah aloja un *spa* que combina lo local con lo oriental y que fue concebido por la firma especializada ESPA. Construidas con paredes de piedra y techos de paja, las ocho villas del pabellón del *spa* han sido diseñadas según una estética que apela al estilo tradicional como forma de mantener un armonioso vínculo con el entorno.

HOUSE IN **IXTAPA-ZIHUATANEJO**

Enrique Muller // eclectica@prodigy.net.mx // © Angelo Destefani Hernandez

This house is located on the Grand Coast of Guerrero, Mexico. The balance between architecture and nature is evident in the overall design of the home. The predominant use of white, complemented by dark woods and accents of color by way of accessories maximizes the sensation of openness and luminosity.

Cette maison se trouve sur la Grande Côte du Guerrero, au Mexique. L'équilibre entre nature et architecture se retrouve dans l'ensemble du design. La prédominance du blanc, associée à des bois foncés et à quelques touches de couleurs apportées par les accessoires, optimise la sensation d'ouverture et de luminosité.

Questa casa si trova nella zona di Costa Grande de Guerrero, in Messico. L'equilibrio tra architettura e natura appare evidente nel progetto generale della casa. L'uso predominante del bianco, integrato da legni scuri e accenti di colore negli accessori, potenzia al massimo la sensazione di apertura e luminosità.

Dieses Haus, dessen Design das harmonische Gleichgewicht von Architektur und Natur ausstrahlt, steht im Gebiet Costa Grande im mexikanischen Bundesstaat Guerrero. Der vorherrschende Einsatz der Farbe Weiß in Verbindung mit dunklen Hölzern und einigen farbigen Accessoires verstärkt die Wirkung von Offenheit und Helligkeit.

Dit huis ligt aan de Costa Grande van Guerrero, in Mexico. De balans tussen architectuur en natuur is duidelijk in het algemene ontwerp van de woning. Het overheersende gebruik van wit, aangevuld met zwart hout en kleuraccenten als accessoires, vergroot het gevoel van openheid en lichtheid.

Esta casa se ubica en la Costa Grande de Guerrero, en México. El equilibrio entre arquitectura y naturaleza es patente en el diseño general de la vivienda. El uso predominante del blanco, complementado por maderas oscuras y acentos de color en forma de accesorios, potencia al máximo la sensación de amplitud y luminosidad.

AMAN-I-KHÁS

Jean-Michel Gathy // www.denniston.com.my // © Amanresorts

Aman-i-Khás is a wilderness camp located in a rugged brushwood forest on the fringes of Ranthambore National Park. Combining the Sanskrit word for 'peace' with the Hindi word for 'special', Aman-i-Khás offers accommodation in 10 luxury air-conditioned tents each with soaring canopies draped in the Moghul style.

Aman-i-Khás est un camp naturel situé dans une savane entourant le Parc national de Ranthambore. Associant le mot sanscrit signifiant « paix » et le mot hindi pour « spécial », Aman-i-Khás comporte 10 tentes luxueuses disposant de l'air conditionné ; chacune d'entre elles est ornée de voiles drapées à la façon moghole.

Aman-i-Khás è un campo ubicato in un aspro sottobosco a poca distanza dal Parco Nazionale Ranthambore. Aman-i-Khás, che combina il termine sanscrito che significa «pace» con quello Hindi che significa «speciale», offre sistemazioni in dieci lussuose tende dotate di aria condizionata, ognuna con imponente letto a baldacchino arricchito da drappeggi in stile Moghul.

Aman-i-Khás – eine Kombination des Sanskrit-Wortes für „Frieden" und des Hindi-Begriffs für „besonders" – ist ein Camp in einem wilden Buschwald am Rande des Ranthambore-Nationalparks. Es bietet seinen Gästen Unterkunft in 10 klimatisierten Luxuszelten mit eleganten Baldachinen, die im Mogulstil drapiert sind.

Aman-i-Khás is een kampement in de wildernis, gelegen in een woest kreupelbos aan de rand van Nationaal Park Ranthambore. Het Sanskriet woord voor 'vrede' wordt gecombineerd met het Hindi woord voor 'speciaal', Aman-i-Khás biedt accommodatie in 10 luxe tenten met air-conditioning en baldakijnen, gestoffeerd in de Moghul stijl.

Aman-i-Khás es un campamento en plena naturaleza ubicado en un escarpado bosque de maleza en los confines del Parque Nacional de Ranthambore. Combinando el término sánscrito de «paz» con la palabra hindi para «especial», el Aman-i-Khás ofrece alojamiento en diez tiendas de lujo con aire acondicionado, cada una de ellas con altísimos baldaquines drapeados al estilo mogol.

PORTMAN RESIDENCE

Prima Design // www.designprima.co.uk // © Giorgio Baroni

This spectacular loft is located in Tribeca, a fashionable borough in the avant-garde of culture. East meets West in this residence that exemplifies of elegance and style, and opts for a minimalist look complemented by a collection of Asian antiques. Furniture is limited to the essential, always harmonizing with the art collection that combines Buddha statues with a painting by Chagall.

Ce loft spectaculaire se trouve à Tribeca, un des quartiers les plus à la mode pour être à l'avant-garde culturelle. L'orient et l'occident s'unissent dans cette demeure avec élégance et style, au travers de l'engouement pour l'esthétique minimaliste et d'une collection d'antiquités asiatiques. Le mobilier est réduit au minimum et s'harmonise à la collection d'art, qui conjugue statues de Bouddha et un cadre de Chagall.

Questo spettacolare loft si trova a Tribeca, uno dei quartieri più di moda, per trovarsi all'avanguardia culturale. Oriente ed occidente si fondono in questa casa con eleganza e stile, perché abbina il gusto per l'estetica minimalista ed una collezione d'antichità asiatiche. I mobili sono minimi e in perfetta armonia con la collezione d'arte, che sposa statue di Budda con una tela di Chagall.

Dieses spektakuläre Loft liegt in Tribeca, einem der beliebtesten Viertel der kulturellen Avantgarde. Morgenland und Abendland vereinen sich in dieser stilvollen Wohnung, die gekennzeichnet ist durch die Vorliebe für die minimalistische Ästhetik und eine Kollektion asiatischer Antiquitäten. Das spärliche Mobiliar harmoniert mit der Kunstsammlung, die Buddhastatuetten, aber auch ein Bild von Chagall umfasst.

Deze spectaculaire loft bevindt zich in Tribeca, een van de populairste en modernste wijken van het moment. Het oosten en westen komen elegant en stijlvol samen in deze woning, aangezien de minimalistische esthetiek samengaat met een Aziatische antiekverzameling. Het meubilair is minimalistisch en vormt een harmonieus geheel met de kunstcollectie, waarin Boeddhabeelden met een schilderij van Chagall worden gecombineerd.

Este espectacular *loft* se encuentra en Tribeca, uno de los barrios más de moda por estar a la vanguardia cultural. Oriente y occidente se funden en esta vivienda con elegancia y estilo, puesto que confluyen en ella el gusto por la estética minimalista y una colección de antigüedades asiáticas. El mobiliario es mínimo y armoniza con la colección de arte, que combina estatuas de Buda con un cuadro de Chagall.

SYRIE-MANSOURYA

Anne Judet, Catherine Le Chevallier // © Jean-Pierre Gabriel

The Syrie is an impressive hotel whose architecture includes Arabian components that are reminiscent of palaces and mosques. The use of horseshoe and semicircular arches and vaulted ceilings in some of the rooms stands out here. The interior rooms are dominated by Arabian adornments on the walls, called laceria. The bedrooms were decorated in Arabian style.

Le Syrie est un hôtel impressionnant qui, fondé sur une architecture aux composantes arabes, rappelle un palais ou une petite mosquée. Dans certaines pièces, le regard est attiré par la présence d'arcs en fer à cheval et en plein cintre ainsi que par les plafonds voûtés. Dans les salons intérieurs, l'ornementation arabesque, appelée « entrelacs », prédomine sur les murs. Les chambres sont décorées dans le style arabe.

Il Syrie è un impressionante hotel caratterizzato da un'architettura arabeggiante che ricorda un palazzo o una moschea. Notevoli, in alcuni ambienti, gli archi a ferro di cavallo e a tutto sesto e i soffitti a volta. Nelle sale interne predomina la decorazione arabescata delle pareti, chiamata lacería. Le stanze, decorate in stile arabo.

Das Syrie ist ein beeindruckendes Hotel. Es beruht auf einer Bauweise mit arabischen Komponenten, die an einen Palast oder eine Moschee erinnern. Bemerkenswert ist die Verwendung von Hufeisenbögen und Halbkreisbögen sowie die gewölbten Decken in einigen der Räume. In den inneren Wohnräumen überwiegen die arabischen Wandornamente, die sogenannte „lacería". Die Schlafzimmer wurden in arabischem Stil dekoriert.

El Syrie is een indrukwekkend hotel, gebaseerd op een architectuur met Arabische componenten. Opvallend is het gebruik van hoefijzer- en ronde bogen en de gewelfde plafonds van enkele vertrekken. In de salons heeft de arabeske versiering van de wanden de overhand, genaamd «vlechtwerk». De kamers zijn ingericht in Arabische stijl.

El Syrie es un impresionante hotel basado en una arquitectura con componentes arábigos. Destaca el uso del arco de herradura y de medio punto y los techos abovedados en algunas de las estancias. En los salones interiores predomina la ornamentación arabesca de las paredes, llamada «lacería». Las habitaciones fueron decoradas según el estilo árabe.

W RETREAT & SPA

Ecoid // www.ecoid.com // © W Retreat & Spa

Peace, silence, beauty and simple elegance merge to create the aura this Away Spa at the W Retreat & Spa emits. Situated in the Indian Ocean opposite a coral reef, the retreat is built on a floating teak platform, its design a mix of traditional architecture and modern lines with nature at the forefront.

Paix, silence, beauté et élégance simple façonnent la personnalité de cet Away Spa situé dans l'hôtel W Retreat & Spa, au bord de l'océan Indien, face à une barrière de corail. Construit sur une plateforme flottante en teck, son style conjugue architecture traditionnelle et lignes épurées contemporaines, au beau milieu d'une nature jouant un rôle fondamental.

Pace, silenzio, bellezza ed eleganza semplice definiscono la personalità di questo Away Spa ubicato presso l'hotel W Retreat & Spa, affacciato sull'Oceano Indiano davanti a una barriera corallina. Costruito su una piattaforma galleggiante di teak, il progetto fonde l'architettura tradizionale con uno stile dalle linee pure e contemporanee in cui la natura ha un ruolo essenziale.

Ruhe, Frieden, Schönheit und schlichte Eleganz prägen den Charakter des Away Spa im Hotel W Retreat & Spa, das am Ufer des Indischen Ozeans vor einem Korallenriff gelegen ist. Das Spa, das sich auf einer schwimmenden Plattform aus Teakholz befindet, spiegelt eine Mischung aus traditioneller Architektur und einem zeitgenössischen Stil mit klaren Linien wider, in der die Natur die Hauptrolle spielt.

Rust, stilte, schoonheid en eenvoudige elegantie vormen de persoonlijkheid van deze Away Spa, gelegen in het W Retreat & Spa hotel, gelegen aan de oevers van de Indische Oceaan, tegenover het koraalrif. Het ontwerp, gebouwd op een drijvend teakhouten platform, is een mengeling van de traditionele architectuur met een stijl van pure en eigentijdse lijnen waarin de natuur een belangrijke rol speelt.

Paz, silencio, belleza y elegancia sencilla conforman la personalidad de este Away Spa ubicado en el hotel W Retreat & Spa, que se halla en el océano Índico, frente a un arrecife de coral. Construido sobre una plataforma flotante de teca, su diseño es una mezcla de arquitectura tradicional con un estilo de líneas puras y contemporáneo en el que la naturaleza tiene un papel fundamental.

RED ROOM

Anda Andrei // www.ianschragercompany.com // © Pep Escoda

The combination of classic and modern balances the design in an atemporal environment: a pool table covered in stainless steel and upholstered in red, chairs in silvery Indian prints, silver trays, and glass chandeliers make for a theatrical environment.

Le mélange de mobilier classique et moderne donne un design harmonieux dans une atmosphère intemporelle : une table de billard plaquée d'acier inoxydable au tapis rouge, des chaises recouvertes de tissage argenté d'Inde, plateaux d'argent ou chandeliers de cristal créent une ambiance théâtrale.

La combinazione di classico e moderno conferisce un equilibrio particolare al design del locale collocandolo in un'atmosfera senza tempo: un tavolo da biliardo rivestito in acciaio inossidabile con tappeto rosso, le sedie con stampe indiane argentate, i vassoi d'argento e i candelabri di vetro creano un ambiente decisamente teatrale.

Durch die ausgewogene Kombination von klassischem und modernem Mobiliar entsteht der Eindruck einer zeitlosen Umgebung: Ein Edelstahl verkleideter Billardtisch mit rotem Bezug, bunt bedruckte Sessel aus Indien, Silbertabletts sowie auch die gläsernen Kronleuchter schaffen eine nahezu theatrale Atmosphäre.

De combinatie van klassieke en moderne meubels brengt evenwicht in het ontwerp, in een tijdloze sfeer: een roestvrij stalen biljarttafel met rood tapijt, stoelen bekleed met zilverkleurige stoffen uit India, zilveren dienbladen en glazen armkandelaars zorgen voor een zeer theatrale sfeer.

La combinación de muebles clásicos y modernos equilibra el diseño en una atmósfera atemporal: una mesa de billar chapada de acero inoxidable con tapiz de color rojo, sillas estampadas con tejidos plateados de la India, bandejas de plata o candelabros de cristal componen un ambiente muy teatral.

EXIT

EXIT

THE GARDENS OF **SKOURA**

Carole Lecomte // www.lesjardinsdeskoura.com // © Jean-Pierre Gabriel

Located in the heart of the Skoura palm grove, this ancient example of traditional architecture offers its guests eight bedrooms decorated according to the Moroccan style, with Arabian carpets and rugs. From the exterior garden one can see the spectacular palm grove that surrounds the building; a true oasis in the middle of the desert.

Située au coeur de la palmeraie de Skoura, cette ancienne propriété d'architecture traditionnelle offre à ses hôtes huit chambres décorées dans le style marocain, entre tapis et tentures arabes. Depuis le jardin extérieur, la vue s'étend sur la palmeraie spectaculaire qui entoure l'édifice, véritable oasis au cœur du désert.

Ubicata nel cuore del palmeto di Skoura, questa antica proprietà dall'architettura tradizionale offre ai suoi ospiti otto stanze decorate in stile marocchino, con tappeti e arazzi arabi. Dal giardino si può ammirare lo spettacolare palmeto che circonda l'edificio, una vera e propria oasi in mezzo al deserto.

Dieses alte Haus in traditioneller Bauweise, mitten im Herzen eines Palmenhains in Skoura gelegen, bietet seinen Gästen 8 Zimmer an, welche nach marrokanischem Stil mit arabischen Teppichen und Wandteppichen geschmückt sind. Vom Garten im Außenbereich erblickt man den Aufsehen erregenden Palmenhain, der das Gebäude umgibt, eine wahre Oase mitten in der Wüste.

Dit oude eigendom, gebouwd volgens de traditionele architectuur, biedt de gasten acht kamers die naar Marokkaanse stijl zijn ingericht, met Arabische vloerkleden en wandtapijten. Vanaf de tuin kan men het spectaculaire palmbos dat het gebouw omringt bewonderen; een authentieke oasis midden in de woestijn.

Situada en el corazón del palmeral de Skoura, esta antigua propiedad de arquitectura tradicional ofrece a sus huéspedes ocho habitaciones decoradas según el estilo marroquí, entre alfombras y tapices árabes. Desde el jardín exterior se puede ver la espectacularidad del palmeral que rodea el edificio, un auténtico oasis en medio del desierto.

GIRNAR

Rajiv Saini & Associates // www.rajivsaini.com // © Courtesy RS+A

Furniture brought over from Vietnam, Nepal, Udaipur and Pondicherry occupies a privileged place in this home in Bombay. The walls display part of the owner's private, contemporary art collection together with tribal wood carvings. Elements inherited from the past and the contemporary art on display create a space with a mix of styles.

Le mobilier originaire du Vietnam, Népal, Udaipur et de Pondichéry est le point de mire de cette demeure de Bombay. Les murs accueillent une partie de la collection privée d'art contemporain du propriétaire à côté de sculptures tribales taillées dans le bois. Les témoins du passé et l'art contemporain exposé créent un espace où les styles se mêlent.

La mobilia, proveniente dal Vietnam, dal Nepal, da Udaipur e da Pondicherry, svolge un ruolo determinante nel design di questa residenza di Bombay. Sulle pareti è esposta una parte della collezione privata di arte contemporanea del proprietario, assieme a sculture di legno intagliato in stile tribale. In questo modo, lo stile degli oggetti appartenenti al passato e quello degli oggetti contemporanei si fonde in un unico spazio.

Die Möbel aus Vietnam, Nepal und Udaipur Pondicherry nehmen einen wichtigen Platz in diesem Wohnhause in Bombay ein. An den Wänden ist ein Teil der Privatsammlung moderner Kunst des Besitzers ausgestellt, sowie auch Stammesskulpturen aus geschnitztem Holz. Die aus der Vergangenheit geerbten Stücke und die ausgestellte Gegenwartskunst befinden sich in einem Raum, in dem sich verschiedene Stile mischen.

Het meubilair is afkomstig uit Vietnam, Nepal, Udaipur en Pondicherry en neemt een belangrijke plaats in in deze woning in Bombay. Aan de wanden hangt een deel van de privé-verzameling eigentijdse kunst van de eigenaar, naast tribale houtsnijwerken. De uit het verleden geërfde elementen en de hedendaagse kunst creëren een ruimte waarin diverse stijlen worden gecombineerd.

El mobiliario traído de Vietnam, Nepal, Udaipur y Pondicherry ocupa un lugar destacado en esta vivienda de Bombay. En las paredes se expone parte de la colección privada de arte contemporáneo del propietario, junto con esculturas tribales de madera tallada. Los elementos heredados del pasado y el arte contemporáneo expuesto crean un espacio en el que se mezclan los estilos.

A PLACE **IN THE SUN**

Owner // © Conrad White/Zapaimages

This house, situated in the west of Ibiza, is in keeping with the style of this Balearic island, based on a totally white architectural structure. Neutral colors dominate, together with elegant materials of simple design, carefully selected not to break with the serenity, like the cages that preside over the entrance to the stairway.

Cette maison, située sur la côte ouest d'Ibiza, s'inscrit dans le style des Baléares, basé sur une structure architecturale entièrement blanche. Les couleurs neutres et les matériaux nobles sans détails superflus, ont été soigneusement sélectionnés pour ne pas briser la sérénité, comme les cages devant l'entrée des escaliers.

Situata sulla costa ovest di Ibiza, questa casa completamente bianca segue lo stile architettonico proprio dell'isola. Predominano i colori neutri e i materiali nobili quasi del tutto privi di dettagli, selezionati con cura per non turbare la quiete che trasmette il progetto. Un esempio sono le gabbie poste a presiedere l'accesso alle scale.

Dieses Haus, an der Westküste Ibizas gelegen, ist in einem für die Insel typischen Baustil gehalten – der Architektur in Weiß. Es überwiegen neutrale Farben und edle Materialien mit wenigen Details, welche sorgfältig ausgewählt wurden, um die Ruhe nicht zu brechen, wie z. Bsp. die Käfige vor dem Eingang zu den Treppen.

Dit huis, gelegen aan de westkust van Ibiza, volgt de eigen stijl van de Balearen en is gebaseerd op een helemaal witte architectonische structuur. Neutrale en nobele materialen hebben de bovenhand, en de weinige details zijn zorgvuldig uitgekozen om de rust niet te breken, zoals de vazen aan het begin van de trappen.

Esta casa, situada en la costa oeste de Ibiza, sigue el estilo propio de la isla balear, basado en una estructura arquitectónica totalmente blanca. Predominan los colores neutros y los materiales nobles con escasos detalles, cuidadosamente seleccionados para no romper con la quietud, como las jaulas que presiden la entrada de las escaleras.

JEAN GABIN
LE CLOCHARD
DARRY COWL
GILLES GRANGIER
Indien Interieurs

VILLA **DEL SETTECENTO A POSITANO**

Lazzarini Pickering Architteti // www.lazzarinipickering.com // © Matteo Piazza

The project began with a basic idea: how to integrate the urban context with the architectural wealth and decorative traditions of the original building, which dates back to the 17th century and which formed part of a monastery. The architects knew how to reinterpret the building's monastic function and integrated a contemporary style with Arabic influences from the Amalfi Coast.

Le projet est parti d'une idée de base essentielle : comment intégrer le contexte urbain à la richesse architecturale et aux traditions décoratives de l'édifice original du XVIIe siècle, ancien élément d'un monastère. Les architectes ont su réinterpréter la fonction monacale de l'édifice tout en l'intégrant au style contemporain influencé par les traditions arabes de la côte amalfitaine.

L'idea fondamentale di questo progetto è stata quella di fondere il contesto urbano con la ricchezza dell'architettura e della tradizione decorativa dell'edificio originale, una costruzione del XVII secolo che formava parte di un monastero. Gli architetti hanno saputo dare una nuova interpretazione all'antica funzione religiosa dell'edificio integrando uno stile contemporaneo con le influenze della tradizione araba della costa amalfitana.

Das Projekt ging von folgender Grundidee aus: Wie kann man den urbanen Kontext mit seinem architektonischen Reichtum und die dekorativen Traditionen des Originalbaus aus dem 17. Jhdt. welcher Teil eines Klosters war, miteinander verbinden? Die Architekten verstanden es, die Funktion des Gebäudes als Kloster neuzuerfassen, und integrierten einen zeitgenössischen Stil, mit Einflüssen aus der arabischen Tradition der amalfitanischen Küste.

Dit project heeft als uitgangspunt: hoe kan de stedelijke context geïntegreerd worden binnen de architectonische rijkdom en de decoratieve tradities van het originele gebouw. De architecten zijn erin geslaagd om de functie van klooster van het gebouw opnieuw te interpreteren en hebben een eigentijdse stijl geïntegreerd met invloeden uit de Arabische traditie van de Amalfitaanse kust.

El proyecto partió de una idea básica: cómo integrar el contexto urbano con la riqueza arquitectónica y las tradiciones decorativas del edificio original, datado del siglo XVII y que formó parte de un monasterio. Los arquitectos supieron reinterpretar la función monástica del edificio e integraron el estilo contemporáneo con influencias de la tradición árabe de la costa amalfitana.

CAMP HOWIE HOUSE

Bensley Design Studios // www.bensley.com/html/eng // © Bensley Design Studios

The residence is composed of seven buildings, with three central Thai style pavilions that accommodate the kitchen, the dining room, the main lounge and the bedrooms. The large items of furniture have been designed by the architectural studio and the accessories have been acquired in antique markets from the villages and shops of Thailand, India, Laos and Burma.

L'habitation comporte sept constructions, avec trois pavillons centraux de style thaï qui accueillent la cuisine et la salle à manger, le salon principal et les chambres à coucher. Le design des grands meubles est l'œuvre du bureau d'architecture et les accessoires ont été glanés au marchés d'antiquités des villages et magasins de Thaïlande, Inde, Laos et Birmanie.

La casa è composta da sette edifici con tre padiglioni centrali in stile tai, che accolgono la cucina e la sala da pranzo, il soggiorno principale e le camere da letto. I grandi mobili sono stati progettati dallo studio d'architettura e gli accessori sono stati acquistati in innumerevoli mercati d'antiquariato e negozi nei villaggi della Tailandia, l'India, il Laos e la Birmania.

Das Anwesen besteht aus sieben Gebäuden, darunter drei zentrale Pavillons im thailändischen Stil, die als Küche und Speisezimmer, Hauptsalon sowie Schlafzimmer genutzt werden. Die großzügig geschnittenen Möbel wurden auch vom Architekten entworfen, und die einzigartigen Dekorationsobjekte haben die Besitzer während ihrer zahlreichen Reisen in Thailand, Indien, Laos und Myanmar erworben.

De woning bestaat uit zeven gebouwen met drie centrale paviljoens in Thaise stijl, waarin de keuken en de eetkamer, de hoofdzaal en de slaapkamers zijn ondergebracht. De grote meubels zijn ontworpen door het architectenbureau en de accessoires zijn aangekocht op talrijke antiekmarkten in de dorpen en winkels van Thailand, India, Laos en Birma.

La vivienda se compone de siete edificaciones, con tres pabellones centrales de estilo tailandés que acogen la cocina y el comedor, el salón principal y los dormitorios. Los grandes muebles han sido diseñados por el estudio de arquitectura y los accesorios proceden de innumerables mercados de antigüedades de los pueblos y tiendas de Tailandia, India, Laos y Birmania.

PHINDA ZUKA LODGE

Nicholas Plewman Architects, Chris Brown // nick@plewmanarchitects.co.za // © Craig Fraser

Earthy colors and an obvious fascination the owners have for handcrafts characterize this house, inspired in ethnic decoration. Wicker furniture combines with expertly crafted wood carvings. Different sections of the façade were done with stones, typical to the area, which were put in place without using mortar.

Les couleurs terreuses associées à l'évident engouement des propriétaires pour l'artisanat, caractérisent cette demeure qui s'inspire d'une décoration ethnique. Certains meubles auxiliaires réalisés en rotin se mêlent à des sculptures en bois parfaitement profilées par un ébéniste. Différents pans de la façade ont été élaborés en pierres locales, placées sans avoir recours au mortier.

Colori terrosi e un evidente fascino da parte dei proprietari per l'artigianato caratterizzano questa residenza decorata in stile etnico. Mobili ausiliari di vimini si combinano con sculture in legno rifinite alla perfezione dall'ebanista. Diverse parti della facciata sono composte da pietre tipiche della zona murate a secco.

Erdtöne und eine offensichtliche Faszination der Eigentümer für das Kunsthandwerk prägen den Charakter dieses Wohnhauses, welches von einer ethnischen Dekoration inspiriert ist. Weidenkörbe werden mit perfekten, handgeschnitzten Möbeln kombiniert. Die Teile der Fassade wurden mit für die Umgebung typischen Steinen verkleidet.

Aardekleuren en een duidelijke fascinatie van de eigenaren voor ambachtelijke voorwerpen kenmerken deze woning met een etnische inrichting. Sommige uit rotan vervaardigde bijzetmeubels worden gecombineerd met houtsnijwerken die perfect door een meubelmaker zijn afgewerkt. Verschillende delen van de gevel zijn bewerkt met steensoorten uit de streek.

Los colores terrosos y una evidente fascinación de los propietarios por la artesanía caracterizan esta vivienda inspirada en una decoración étnica. Algunos muebles auxiliares realizados en mimbre se combinan con tallas de madera perfectamente perfiladas por un ebanista. Diferentes tramos de la fachada fueron elaborados con piedras típicas de la zona.

DIPLOMATIC RESIDENCE

Design Worldwide Partnership // www.dwp.com // © Amir Sultan

The formal rooms of the residence have been designed to accommodate the ambassador's personal collection of objects of art. The photographs taken on the European Union representative's trips around Asia transmit the simplicity of the continent's lifestyle. The furniture has been chosen bearing in mind the comfort and aesthetics of this diplomatic showcase and nexus of different cultures.

Les pièces officielles de la résidence ont été conçues pour héberger la collection personnelle d'objets d'art de l'ambassadeur. Les photographies, capturées lors des voyages du représentant de l'Union Européenne à travers l'Asie, transmettent la simplicité du style de vie du continent. Le mobilier a été choisi en tenant compte de la commodité et de l'esthétique de cette vitrine diplomatique, lieu de rencontre de cultures distinctes.

Le stanze formali della residenza sono state progettate per ospitare la collezione personale d'oggetti d'arte dell'ambasciatore. Le fotografie scattate durante i viaggi del rappresentante dell'Unione Europea in Asia trasmettono la semplicità dello stile di vita del continente. L'arredamento è stato scelto pensando alla comodità e l'estetica di questa vetrina diplomatica e nesso d'unione di diverse culture.

Die Räume wurden so entworfen, dass die persönliche Sammlung von Fotografien in den Vordergrund tritt. Gerade in den Fotografien, die während der zahlreichen Reisen des Botschafters entstanden sind, werden dem Betrachter die faszinierende Vielfalt der Regionen und die Einfachheit des asiatischen Lebensstils vermittelt. Das Mobiliar wurde nach Gesichtspunkten ausgewählt, die sowohl den Komfort als auch die Ästhetik und die Funktion dieses Diplomaten-Anwesens berücksichtigen.

De formele vertrekken van de residentie zijn ontworpen om een persoonlijke collectie kunstvoorwerpen, foto's en schilderijen van de ambassadeur in onder te brengen, die daarmee opvallen binnen de ruimte. De foto's, genomen tijdens de reizen van de vertegenwoordiger van de Europese Unie door Azië, geven blijk van de eenvoud van de levensstijl van het continent.

Las estancias formales de la residencia han sido diseñadas para albergar la colección personal de objetos de arte, fotografías y pinturas del embajador, convirtiéndose en la protagonista del espacio. Las fotografías captadas durante los viajes por Asia del representante de la Unión Europea transmiten la simplicidad del estilo de vida del continente. El mobiliario se ha seleccionado teniendo en cuenta la estética y la comodidad de este escaparate diplomático y crisol de culturas.

ANDY WAHLOO

Bruno Caron, Hassan Hajjaj // caronbr@club-internet.fr // © Daniel Nicolas

This snack bar in Paris pays homage to Andy Warhol. Designed by artist Hassan Hajjaj, the result is a space that combines recycled objects with those of Moroccan origin. The originality of this eclectic mix of elements lies not so much in the actual interest of the individual pieces but in their combination with the other objects, which lends the space a unique color and character.

Situé à Paris, ce snack-bar, rend hommage à Andy Warhol. Signé par l'artiste Hassan Hajjaj, l'espace mêle objets recyclés et pièces d'origine marocaine. L'originalité de ce mélange d'éléments éclectiques ne réside pas uniquement dans l'intérêt qu'ils suscitent individuellement, mais davantage dans leur métissage avec le reste des objets, imprimant ainsi à l'espace une couleur et un caractère uniques.

Questo snack bar di Parigi è un omaggio a Andy Warhol. Il disegno dell'artista Hassan Hajjaj crea uno spazio dove si fondono oggetti riciclati con oggetti originari del Marocco. La singolarità di questa combinazione eclettica di elementi risiede non tanto nel valore artistico di ogni singolo oggetto, bensì nella combinazione degli oggetti tra loro, che conferisce allo spazio un colore e un carattere unici.

Diese Snackbar in Paris ist eine Huldigung an Andy Warhol. Das Design stammt von dem Künstler Hassan Hajjaj; das Ergebnis ist ein Raum, in dem wiederverwertete Objekte mit Möbeln marokkanischer Herkunft kombiniert werden. Das Originelle an dieser eklektischen Mischung von Elementen ist nicht so sehr ihr Wert, sondern die Kombination von Einzelstücken mit den restlichen Objekten, was dem Raum eine Farbenpracht und einen speziellen Charakter verleiht.

Deze tapasbar, gelegen in Parijs, is een eerbetoon aan Andy Warhol. Hij is ontworpen door de kunstenaar Hassan Hajjaj en het resultaat is een ruimte waarin gerecyclede voorwerpen zijn gecombineerd met voorwerpen van Marokkaanse origine. De origineelheid van deze eclectische mengeling van elementen is niet zozeer gelegen in het belang van ieder stuk op zich, maar in de combinatie van alle elementen met de rest van de voorwerpen.

Este bar de tapas situado en París rinde homenaje a Andy Warhol. Diseñado por el artista Hassan Hajjaj, el resultado es un espacio que mezcla objetos reciclados con otros de origen marroquí. La originalidad de esta mezcla ecléctica de elementos reside no tanto en el propio interés de cada pieza sino en la combinación de cada una de ellas con el resto de los objetos, lo que dota de un color y carácter único al espacio.

المغرب
Maroc
PRODUIT DU MAROC
PRODUCE OF MOROCCO

SORTIE
CAFES
SAADA
30 KG
midi

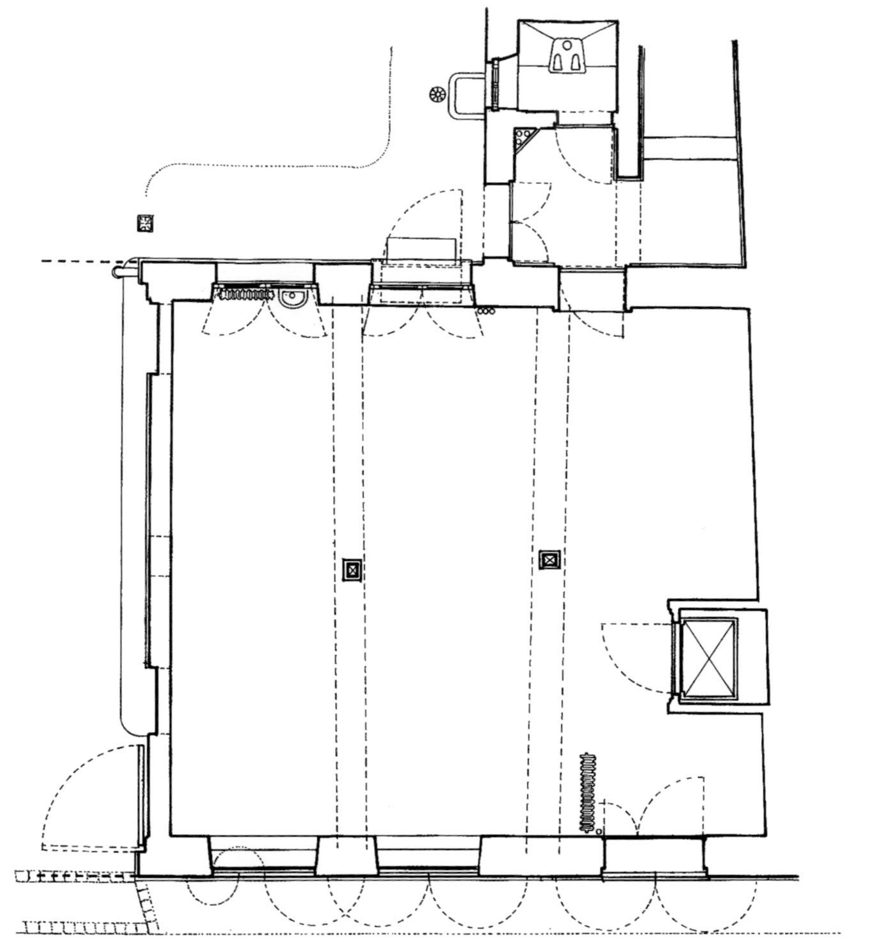

Floor plan

VERANA **IN MEXICO**

Heinz Legler & Veronique Lievre (Owners) // © D. Vorillon/Inside/Cover

One of the premises when taking on the renovation of this house in Mexico was to preserve the local style both in the constructive elements and the decorative details in the interior. Ochre dominates, accentuating the home's rustic style. Decorative motifs have been painted on the walls that are reminiscent of cave paintings.

La réhabilitation de cette demeure, située à Mexico, respecte parfaitement le style local, tant dans les éléments constructifs que dans les détails décoratifs de l'intérieur. La couleur ocre prédomine, accentuant le style rustique de la demeure. Sur les murs, les motifs décoratifs peints rappellent les peintures rupestres dans les grottes.

Una delle premesse del progetto di ristrutturazione di questa residenza situata in Messico è stata quella di conservare lo stile autoctono sia negli elementi costruttivi sia nei dettagli decorativi dell'interno. Il color ocra è predominante e serve a sottolineare lo stile rustico dell'abitazione. Le pareti sono state decorate con motivi che ricordano le pitture rupestri.

Eine der Prämissen bei der Durchführung der Sanierung dieses mexikanischen Wohnhauses war es, den urwüchsigen Stil zu bewahren, sowohl bei den Bauelementen als auch bei den dekorativen Details der Innenräume. Die Ockerfarbe dominiert, wodurch der rustikale Charakter des Hauses betont wird. An den Wänden wurden wirkungsvolle Motive aufgemalt, die an Höhlenmalereien erinnern.

Een van de premissen bij de aanpak van de restauratie van deze in Mexico gelegen woning was het behouden van de autochtone stijl, zowel in de bouwelementen als in de decoratieve details van het interieur. De kleur oker heeft de overhand, waarmee de landelijke stijl van de woning wordt onderstreept. Op de wanden zijn decoratieve motieven geschilderd die doen denken aan rotsschilderingen.

Una de las premisas al emprender la rehabilitación de esta vivienda situada en México fue preservar el estilo autóctono tanto en los elementos constructivos como en los detalles decorativos del interior. Predomina el color ocre, que acentúa el estilo rústico de la vivienda. En las paredes se han pintado motivos decorativos que recuerdan las pinturas rupestres.

METHVEN HOUSE

Michael & Anthea Methven // moonlightandmagic@mweb.co.za // © Craig Fraser

This home seems to have a life of its own. A life size luminous figure of a zebra is a surprising find, which represents a revaluation of the ethnic, modern and somewhat extravagant style. Other details stand out such as the African pictures, fabrics in warm colors, handcrafted objects and rugs with elaborate designs.

Cette demeure semble avoir une vie propre. Le visiteur est surpris par la silhouette d'un zèbre lumineux grandeur nature qui revalorise le style ethnique, moderne et un tant soit peu extravagant. D'autres détails accrochent le regard, à l'instar de portraits africains, tissus aux couleurs chaleureuses, objets artisanaux et tapis aux dessins élaborés.

Sembrerebbe che questa abitazione goda di vita propria. Sorprendente la zebra luminosa di dimensioni naturali che intende rivalorizzare uno stile etnico, moderno e un po' stravagante. Da notare anche altri dettagli, come i ritratti africani, i tessuti in colori caldi, gli oggetti artigianali e i tappeti dai disegni elaborati.

Dieses Wohnhaus scheint ein Eigenleben zu haben. Überraschend ist die Figur eines leuchtenden Zebras in Lebensgröße, was eine Wiederaufwertung des Ethno-Stils, modern und etwas extravagant, darstellt. Hervorzuheben sind weitere Details wie afrikanische Porträts, Stoffe in warmen Farbtönen, Kunsthandwerksstücke und Teppiche mit edlen Mustern.

Deze woning lijkt een eigen leven te leiden. Opvallend is de figuur van een lichtgevende zebra op ware grootte, die een herwaardering van de etnische, moderne en een tikje extravagante stijl vertegenwoordigt. Er zijn andere opvallende details zoals Afrikaanse portretten, stoffen met warme kleuren, ambachtelijke voorwerpen en tapijten met uitgewerkte tekeningen.

Esta vivienda parece tener vida propia. Sorprende la figura de una cebra luminosa de tamaño real que representa una revalorización del estilo étnico, moderno y un tanto extravagante. Destacan otros detalles, como retratos africanos, tejidos con colores cálidos, objetos artesanales y alfombras con elaborados dibujos.

LA XINA

Sandra Tarruella Interioristas // www.sandratarruella.com // © Olga Planas

Textures, colors, aromas, steam from the kitchens, the patina of aged wood, wall lamps in the form of Chinese lanterns, and the symbolism of the dragon lamp, all help to create a Chinese feel in this restaurant without falling into the trap of clichés. For the wall cladding and to separate some of the spaces, Chinese wooden lattices were used. The floor is aged oak.

Les textures, les couleurs, les odeurs, la vapeur des cuisines, la patine vieillie du bois, les lampions utilisés comme éclairage mural et le symbolisme de la lampe dragon de ce restaurant contribuent à l'évocation d'une ambiance chinoise, sans pour autant tomber dans les clichés. Des treillis chinois en bois ont été utilisés pour le revêtement des murs et pour séparer certains espaces. Le parquet est en chêne vieilli.

Materiali, colori, odori, il vapore delle cucine, la patina del legno invecchiato, i lampadari a parete tipo lanterne e il simbolismo della lampada a forma di drago contribuiscono a evocare in questo ristorante un ambiente di ispirazione cinese senza cadere nei luoghi comuni. Per il rivestimento delle pareti e per separare alcuni spazi, sono stati utilizzati dei paraventi cinesi in legno. Il pavimento è in rovere invecchiato.

Texturen, Farben, Düfte, der Dampf aus der Küche, die Patina des Holzes, die lampionartigen Leuchten und die Symbolik der Drachenlampe tragen dazu bei, dass in diesem Restaurant eine echt chinesische Atmosphäre herrscht, ohne jedoch klassische Klischees zu bedienen. Für die Wandverkleidung und zur Abtrennung einzelner Bereiche wurden chinesische Holzjalousien verwendet, der Fußboden ist aus gealtertem Eichenholz.

Texturen, kleuren, geuren, keukendampen, de verkleuring van het hout, wandlampen in de vorm van lampionnen en het symbolisme van de drakenlamp, dragen bij aan de Chinese sfeer die in het restaurant heerst, zonder in cliché's te vervallen. Voor het bekleden van de wanden en om enkele ruimtes van elkaar af te scheiden, is gebruik gemaakt van Chinese houten jaloezieën. Het restaurant heeft een verouderd eikenhouten vloer.

Texturas, colores, olores, el vapor de las cocinas, la pátina envejecida de la madera, las lámparas de pared a modo de farolillo y el simbolismo de la lámpara dragón contribuyen a evocar en este restaurante un ambiente chino sin caer en los tópicos. Para el revestimiento de las paredes, y para separar algunos espacios, se han utilizado celosías chinas de madera. El pavimento es de roble envejecido.

LA★XINA
RESTAURANT
ROBERT ORIENTAL
BARCELONA
TRAGALUZ

BARBAROS BAY KEMPINSKI

Sinan Kafadar/Metex Design Group // www.metexdesign.com // © Jorg Sundermann

Located in the picturesque Barbaros Bay, the Hotel Kempinski boasts a privileged view over the Aegean Sea's turquoise waters and golden sandy beaches. Its contemporary design is adapted to the natural features of the site and alludes to the traditional architecture of this region, characterised by multiculturalism.

Situé dans la baie pittoresque des Barbares, l'hôtel Kempinski bénéficie d'une vue privilégiée sur la mer Égée aux eaux turquoise et aux plages de sable doré. Son style moderne s'adapte à la géographie de l'emplacement et fait allusion à l'architecture traditionnelle de cette région caractérisée par la multiculturalité.

Ubicato nella pittoresca Baia di Barbaros, l'Hotel Kempinski gode di una vista privilegiata sul mar Egeo con le sue acque turchesi e le spiagge di sabbia dorata. Il design moderno si adatta alla geografia del luogo e richiama l'architettura tradizionale della regione, caratterizzata dalla multiculturalità.

In der malerischen Bucht von Barbaros gelegen, erfreut sich das Hotel Kempinski eines privilegierten Ausblicks über die Ägäis mit ihrem türkisblauen Gewässern und goldenen Sandstränden. Sein modernes Design passt sich nahtlos in die Landschaft seines Standortes ein und ist Augenzwinkern zur traditionellen Architektur dieser durch Multikulturalität geprägten Region.

Het in de pittoreske Barbaros Bay gelegen Hotel Kempinski biedt een geprivilegieerd uitzicht over de Egeïsche Zee met zijn turkooisblauwe zee en gouden zandstranden. Het moderne ontwerp is aangepast aan de geografie van de locatie en verwijst naar de traditionele streekarchitectuur, die gekenmerkt wordt door zijn multiculturele kenmerken.

Situado en la pintoresca Bahía de Barbaros, el Hotel Kempinski goza de una vista privilegiada sobre el mar Egeo de agua turquesa y playas de arena dorada. Su diseño moderno se adapta a la geografía del emplazamiento y alude a la tradicional arquitectura de esta región caracterizada por la multiculturalidad.

WILTSHIRE HOUSE

Anouska Hempel Design // www.anouskahempeldesign.com // © Andrew Lawson

The elegant interior design of the house has been designed to be adaptable to all seasons of the year. To do this a variety of styles, colors and textures were chosen in an impressive selection of furniture acquired from different parts of the world. The final result is a harmonic ensemble created from a deliberate union of the Oriental and the European. The communal rooms present Chinese furniture, with marked geometry and contrasts of red and black.

L'élégant aménagement intérieur de l'habitation a été conçu pour qu'il s'adapte à toutes les époques de l'année. Pour ce faire, le mobilier impressionnant glané dans les différents coins du monde, se décline dans une variété de styles, couleurs et textures. Le résultat final affiche un ensemble harmonieux, conjuguant délibérément l'oriental et l'européen. Les chambres communes présentent des meubles de style chinois avec une géométrie et des contrastes de rouge et noir bien prononcés.

L'elegante disegno degli interni della casa è stato concepito per renderla adatta a tutte le epoche dell'anno. Per questo sono stati scelti vari stili, colori e texture per l'impressionante arredamento acquistato in varie parti del mondo. Il risultato finale è un armonico insieme costruito partendo dalla deliberata comunione tra stile orientale ed europeo. Le stanze comuni mostrano mobili di origine cinese, di marcata geometria, e contrasti di rosso e nero.

Die elegante Inneneinrichtung des Hauses wurde für einen Aufenthalt während des gesamten Jahres geschaffen. Die Vielfalt der Stile, Farben und Texturen macht die gelungene Mischung aus östlichen und westlichen Einflüssen deutlich. In den Gemeinschaftsräumen finden sich chinesische Möbel mit ausgeprägten geometrischen Formen und Kontrasten in Rot und Schwarz.

Het elegante interieurontwerp van de woning is zo uitgedacht dat het kan worden aangepast aan alle jaargetijden. De veelzijdigheid van stijlen, kleuren en texturen komt overeen met een weloverwogen congregatie tussen het oosterse en het Europese. In de gemeenschappelijke vertrekken staat meubilair van Chinese origine, met een duidelijke geometrie en rood-zwart contrasten.

El elegante diseño interior de la vivienda ha sido concebido para que se adaptase a todas las épocas del año. La variedad de estilos, colores y texturas responde a una deliberada comunión entre lo oriental y lo europeo. Las estancias comunes presentan mobiliario de origen chino, de marcada geometría y contrastes de rojo y negro.

NILAYA HERMITAGE

Dean D'Cruz // www.mozaic.in // © Nilaya Hermitage

The blue domed hall furnished with silk covered mattresses and cushions lend it an atmosphere reminiscent of Rajashtani palaces. Each room is an exercise of style. The design is an eclectic jumble of Mogul, Mediterranean, Portuguese, Spanish influences, mixed with touches of Hindu temple.

Le hall bleu en forme de dôme, décoré de coussins et de matelas recouverts de soie, confère à ce lieu une atmosphère rappelant les palais du Rajasthan. Chaque chambre est un exercice de style. Le design est un mélange éclectique d'influences mogholes, méditerranéennes, portugaises et espagnoles, associées à des allures de temple hindou.

L'ingresso a cupola nei toni del blu arredato con materassi e cuscini ricoperti di seta ricrea un'atmosfera che ricorda i palazzi del Rajasthan. Ogni camera è un esercizio di stile. Il design è una miscela eclettica di influenze mediterranee, mogul, portoghesi e spagnole cui si aggiungono elementi tipici dei templi Hindu.

Die blaue Halle mit Kuppeldach wurde mit Matratzen und Kissen mit Seidenbezügen ausgestattet, um eine Atmosphäre zu schaffen, die an die Paläste des Rajasthan erinnert. Jedes Zimmer sprüht nur so von besonderem Stil. Das Design ist eine interessante Mischung aus dem Mogulstil mit mediterranen, portugiesischen und spanischen Einflüssen sowie Details eines Hindu-Tempels.

De blauwe, gewelfde hal, ingericht met met zijde beklede matrassen en kussens, geven het een sfeer die doet denken aan die van Rajashtani paleizen. Iedere kamer is een stijloefening. Het ontwerp is een eclectische mengelmoes van Mogul, Mediterrane, Portugese en Spaanse invloeden, gemengd met kenmerken van hindoetempels.

El vestíbulo con cúpula azul parcialmente amueblado con colchones y cojines forrados de seda crea una atmósfera con reminiscencias a los palacios del Rajastán. Cada estancia es un ejercicio de estilo. El diseño es una mezcla ecléctica de influencias mogoles, mediterráneas, portuguesas y españolas, combinadas con toques de templo hindú.

COMO SHAMBHALA ESTATE

Cheong Yew Kuan/Area Designs // area@indo.net.id // © Como Resorts and Hotels

The Estate was conceived and designed as a centre for spiritual and holistic healing. The setting, dominated by a waterfall, forests, paddy fields and misty mountains, has an almost mystical beauty. The area is famous for its springs whose waters have beneficial health properties.

L'Estate est aménagé et conçu comme un centre de cure spirituelle et holistique. Le cadre, dominé par une cascade, des forêts, des champs de riz et des montagnes embrumées, génère une scène à la beauté presque mystique. La zone est réputée pour ses sources d'eau auxquelles des propriétés bénéfiques pour la santé sont attribuées.

L'Estate è concepito e progettato come un centro di cura spirituale e olistica. L'ambiente circostante, dominato da una cascata, boschi, campi di riso e montagne avvolte nella nebbia, crea uno scenario di bellezza quasi mistica. La zona è famosa per le sorgenti a cui sono attribuite proprietà curative.

Das Estate wurde als spirituelles und ganzheitliches Heilzentrum konzipiert und entworfen. Die von einem Wasserfall, Wäldern, Reisfeldern und in Nebel gehüllten Bergen geprägte Umgebung schafft ein fast mythisches Szenarium der Anmut. Die Region ist für ihre Heilquellen mit anerkanntem Gesundheitsnutzen berühmt.

El Estate is bedacht en ontworpen als een spiritueel en holistisch kuuroord. De omgeving, waarin een waterval, bossen, rijstvelden en in mist omhulde bergen centraal staan, creëert een prachtige, haast mystieke achtergrond. De streek is bekend door zijn bronnen waaraan voor de gezondheid positieve eigenschappen worden toegeschreven.

El Estate está concebido y diseñado como un centro de cura espiritual y holística. El entorno, dominado por una cascada, bosques, campos de arroz y montañas envueltas en niebla, crea un escenario de belleza casi mística. La zona es famosa por los manantiales a los que se les reconoce propiedades beneficiosas para la salud.

PERFECT HOSTS

Saint Dizier Design // www.saintd.com // © Mary Nichols

This residence is located on Big Island, the largest of the Hawaii islands. The unusual entrance to the house consists of a wooden walkway that links the various pavilions that are surrounded by water, creating a fresh summer feel. The architecture and interior design are reminiscent of typical Hawaiian huts, enhanced with rich materials and decorative elements that magnify their elegance.

Cette résidence est située sur Big Island, une des îles de l'archipel de Hawaï. L'accès, remarquable, à la maison se fait par une passerelle de bois qui unit les différents pavillons. L'eau circule entre eux, conférant une ambiance estivale rafraîchissante. L'architecture et la décoration rappellent les cabanes hawaïennes, mais ici réalisée avec des matériaux précieux et des éléments de décoration qui exaltent l'élégance du style.

Questa residenza si trova a Big Island, una delle isole dell'arcipelago delle Hawai. Da notare l'accesso alla casa, che avviene mediante una passerella in legno che unisce i diversi padiglioni. L'acqua circola placida tra questi creando un ambiente estivo e rinfrescante. L'architettura e l'arredamento ricordano quelli delle capanne hawaiane, ma con materiali e oggetti di arredo che accentuano uno stile volutamente elegante.

Das Haus liegt auf Big Island, einer der Inseln des Hawaii-Archipels. Auffällig ist der Zugang zum Haus über einen hölzernen Steg, der die einzelnen Pavillons miteinander verbindet. Darunter fließt Wasser und erfrischt die Luft. Architektur und Einrichtung erinnern an die hawaiianischen Hütten, obwohl der einheimische Baustil hier mit wertvollen Materialien und dekorativen Elementen veredelt wurde.

Deze woning ligt op Big Island, een van de eilanden van de archipel Hawaï. Opvallend is dat men toegang tot de woning heeft via een houten loopbrug, die de verschillende paviljoens met elkaar verbindt. Het water stroomt daar tussen door en zorgt voor een verfrissende zomerse sfeer. De architectuur en de inrichting doen denken aan die van de Hawaïaanse hutten, maar met rijke materialen en decoratieve elementen die de elegantie van de stijl benadrukken.

Esta residencia está situada en Big Island, una de las islas del archipiélago de Hawái. Destaca la entrada a la casa, que se hace a través de una pasarela de madera que une los diferentes pabellones. El agua circula entre ellos y proporciona un ambiente estival refrescante. La arquitectura y la decoración recuerdan a las cabañas hawaianas, pero con ricos materiales y elementos decorativos que realzan la elegancia del estilo.

FOLEY AND CORINNA

Hut Sachs Studio // www.hutsachs.com // © Martin Albert

Situated in the heart of New York's Lower East Side, Foley and Corinna is characterized by a neo-hippie style which is in keeping with the vintage clothing on display. The result of this collaboration are walls decorated with illustrations that evoke a dreamlike reality, combined with the Moroccan style ceramic collage, the restored furniture and the clothes.

Implanté au coeur du Lower East Side de New York, Foley and Corinna se caractérisent par un style néo-hippie correspondant tout à fait aux vêtements vintage exposés. Il en résulte des murs décorés d'illustrations évoquant une réalité onirique, associés au collage des céramiques de style marocain, au mobilier restauré et aux vêtements.

Situata nel cuore del Lower East Side di New York, la boutique Foley and Corinna è caratterizzata da uno stile neohippy che ben si sposa con i capi di abbigliamento vintage esposti. Ne sono risultate pareti con decorazioni che evocano una realtà onirica, combinate con il collage delle ceramiche in stile marocchino, i mobili restaurati e gli abiti in esposizione.

Mitten im Herzen der Lower East Side von New York gelegen, zeichnet sich Foley and Corinna durch seinen Neo-Hippie-Stil aus, welcher äußerst gut zu der dort angebotenen Vintage-Kleidung passt. Das Resultat sind Wände, geschmückt mit Bildern, die an eine Traumwelt erinnern, in Kombination mit einer collage aus Keramik in marokkanischem Stil, restaurierten Möbeln und Kleidungsstücken.

Gelegen in het hart van de Lower East Side van New Cork, Foley and Corinna wordt gekenmerkt door een neo-hippiestijl, geheel in overeenstemming met de vintage kleding in de etalages. Dit uit zich in wanden, die versierd zijn met illustraties die een droomrealiteit in herinnering brengen, gecombineerd met een collage van keramiek in Marokkaanse stijl, gerestaureerd meubilair en de kleding.

Localizada en el corazón del Lower East Side de Nueva York, Foley and Corinna se caracteriza por un estilo *neo-hippie* muy acorde con la ropa *vintage* expuesta. El resultado fueron unas paredes decoradas con ilustraciones que evocan una realidad onírica, combinadas con el collage de las cerámicas de estilo marroquí, el mobiliario restaurado y la ropa.

WOLF

DRAGON-I

India Mahdavi // www.india-mahdavi.com // © Dragon-i

The decorating of the Dragon-i is based on the fusion of Chinese and Japanese traditions, Oriental mysticism, aesthetic minimalism and beauty. The interior decorating includes red phoenix lamps in prints, low sofas in velvety felt and other objects with a Chinese or Japanese aesthetic. The bathroom has a silver mosaic and there is a huge bamboo bird cage on the terrace.

La décoration est basée sur la fusion entre les traditions chinoise et japonaise, le mysticisme oriental, le minimalisme esthétique et la beauté. La décoration intérieure est dominée par des lampes rouge phénix recouvertes d'imprimés, des banquettes en peluche et d'autres objets typiques de l'esthétique chinoise et japonaise. En outre, les toilettes sont en mosaïque argentée et l'entrée de la terrasse est ornée d'une cage à oiseaux fabriquée en bambou.

Gli arredi si basano sulla fusione tra tradizione cinese e giapponese, mistica orientale, minimalismo estetico e bellezza. Gli arredi interni sono composti da lampadari rosso fenice arricchiti da stampe, divani bassi di peluche e altri oggetti che richiamano un'estetica cinese e giapponese; inoltre il bagno è realizzato in mosaico color argento e all'ingresso della terrazza è stata installata un'enorme gabbia d'uccelli in bambù.

Die Dekoration basiert auf der Fusion der chinesischen und japanischen Tradition und der orientalischen Mystik mit ästhetischem Minimalismus. Die Innenausstattung umfasst knallrote, bedruckte Lampen, niedrige Plüschsofas und andere Objekte, die an die chinesische und japanische Ästhetik angelehnt sind. Die Toiletten sind mit silberfarbenem Mosaik geschmückt und am Zugang zur Terrasse wurde ein riesiger Vogelkäfig aus Bambus platziert.

De inrichting is gebaseerd op de fusie tussen Chinese en Japanse tradities, oosterse mystiek, esthetisch minimalisme en schoonheid. Het interieur is ingericht met lampen met opdruk van fenix rood, lage velours divans en andere voorwerpen die behoren tot de Chinese en Japanse esthetiek. Bovendien is de badkamer van verzilverd mozaïek en is bij de toegang naar het terras een enorme bamboe vogelkooi geïnstalleerd.

La decoración está basada en la fusión de las tradiciones china y japonesa, la mística oriental, el minimalismo estético y la belleza. La decoración interior contempla lámparas de rojo fénix de estampados impresos, sofás bajos de felpa y otros objetos pertenecientes a una estética china y japonesa; además, el cuarto de baño es de mosaico plateado y en la entrada de la terraza se ha instalado una enorme jaula para pájaros hecha con bambú.

ZEAVOLA SPA

Amata Luphaiboon/Department of Architecture Co. Ltd // dept.of.arch@gmail.com // © Noppatad Leerasettakorn

Inspired by the wonders and essence of rural Thailand, the spa at Zeavola boutique resort merges vibrant colors, and natural aromas with the advantages of an ancient culture devoted to rejuvenating the body and nourishing the soul and spirit. The 650-square-foot cabins are decorated with traditional textiles and boast private gardens where showers can be taken in the fresh air.

Inspiré des charmes et de l'essence de la Thaïlande rurale, le spa de l'hôtel Zeavola réunit les couleurs vives, les arômes naturels et les bienfaits d'une culture millénaire pour rajeunir le corps et nourrir l'âme et l'esprit. Les cases de 60 m² sont décorées de tissus traditionnels et donnent sur un jardin privé dans lequel une douche est aménagée.

Ispirato al fascino e all'essenza della Tailandia rurale, il centro benessere dell'hotel Zeavola riunisce i colori vivaci, gli aromi naturali e i benefici di una cultura millenaria per ringiovanire il corpo e alimentare l'anima e lo spirito. Le capanne, ciascuna di 60 m², sono arredate con tessuti tradizionali e dispongono di giardino privato in cui è possibile fare una doccia all'aria aperta.

Das vom besonderen Charme des ländlichen Thailands inspirierte Spa des Hotels Zeavola vereint kräftige Farben, natürliche Aromen und die Vorzüge einer jahrtausendealten Kultur, um den Körper zu verjüngen und Seele und Geist zu nähren. Die 60 m² Hütten sind mit traditionellen Stoffen geschmückt und warten mit einem Privatgarten auf, in dem die Gäste unter freiem Himmel duschen können.

In de spa van hotel Zeavole, die geïnspireerd is op de charme en essentie van het Thaise platteland komen de vibrerende kleuren, natuurlijke aroma's en de voordelen van een eeuwenoude cultuur om het lichaam te verjongen en geest te voeden, samen. De hutten van 60 m² zijn ingericht met traditionele stoffen en hebben een privé-tuin waar men in de open lucht kan douchen.

Inspirado en los encantos y la esencia de la Tailandia rural, el *spa* del hotel Zeavola reúne los colores vibrantes, los aromas naturales y las ventajas de una cultura milenaria para rejuvenecer el cuerpo, y alimentar el alma y el espíritu. Las cabañas, de 60 m² cada una, están decoradas con tejidos tradicionales, y cuentan con un jardín privado donde es posible tomar una ducha al aire libre.

Comfort
Energizing
Sensual

GEOMÉTRICAS THERMAL SPA

Germán del Sol // www.germandelsol.cl // © Guy Wemborne

These hot springs set amidst the Villarrica National Park, offer new sensations in outdoor bathing. The visitor is immersed in the cool shade of the dense surrounding forest in the summer and the snow and rain in winter. The baths are taken in any of the seventeen stone wells spread along the 1,500-foot piece of land in the midst of nature. These wells and which are reached via a red-stained coihue-wood walkway.

Ces thermes, implantés au cœur d'un parc national, sont le lieu idéal pour goûter au plaisir de la baignade en plein air, au milieu de la fraîcheur de la forêt en été ou sous la pluie et la neige en hiver. Les bains sont pris dans l'un des 17 puits en pierre disséminés sur les 450 m de terrain au cœur de la nature, auxquels on accède au moyen d'une passerelle en bois de hêtre de Magellan teint en rouge.

In queste terme inserite all'interno di un parco nazionale è possibile sperimentare il piacere di fare il bagno all'aperto in mezzo al fresco bosco in estate, o sotto la pioggia e la neve in inverno. È possibile fare il bagno in una delle 17 piscine di pietra sparse in 450 m di terreno, immerse nella natura, raggiungibili attraverso una passerella di legno di coihué dipinto di rosso.

In diesen Thermen inmitten eines Nationalparks kommt man in den Genuss des Badens unter freiem Himmel, umgeben vom erfrischen kühlen Wald im Sommer und von Regen und Schnee im Winter. Gebadet wird in einem der 17 steinernen Becken, die sich in der 450 m langen Anlagen erstrecken und über einen rot lasierten Steg aus Coigue-Holz zu erreichen sind.

In deze thermen, gelegen temidden van een nationaal park, kan men ervaren hoe het is om in de openlucht te baden, genietend van de frisheid van het bos, of het nu in de zomer is, in de regen, of 's winters in de sneeuw. De baden zijn aangelegd in enkele van de 17 stenen bronnen die over een oppervlak van 450 m verspreid liggen, midden in de natuur, en die men bereikt via een roodgeverfde coihué houten passerelle.

En estas termas construidas en un parque nacional se puede experimentar el placer de bañarse al aire libre, en medio del frescor del bosque, si es verano, o bajo la lluvia y la nieve en invierno. Los baños se realizan en alguno de los 17 pozos de piedra diseminados a lo largo de 450 m de terreno en medio de la naturaleza, a los que se llega por una pasarela de madera de coihué teñido de rojo.

RESIDENCE IN **PASADENA**

KAA Design Group // www.kaadesigngroup.com // © Pizzi and Thompson

This house is an excellent example of the Spanish colonial style of southern California. Built between 1915 and 1918, it is part of what was originally a large villa that was later subdivided. After being remodeled several times over the years, the owners decided to recover its original spirit. The elegant and exclusive materials used in the décor accentuate the beauty of the interiors.

Cette maison est un excellent exemple de style colonial espagnol du sud de la Californie. Construite entre 1915 et 1918, est la maison une partie de la ferme d'origine qui a été ultérieurement divisée. Au fil des années, elle a subit diverses restaurations jusqu'à ce que les derniers propriétaires aient décidé de récupérer l'esprit initial. Les élégants et nobles matériaux utilisés pour la décoration subliment la beauté des intérieurs.

Questa casa rappresenta un magnifico esempio dello stile coloniale spagnolo del sud della California; edificata tra il 1915 e il 1918, è solo una parte della tenuta originale che è stata successivamente suddivisa. Nel corso degli anni, l'abitazione è stata soggetta a diverse ristrutturazioni fino a che gli ultimi proprietari decisero di recuperarne lo spirito originario. I materiali, eleganti e nobili, adoperati per arredare la casa accentuano la bellezza degli interni.

Dieses zwischen 1915 und 1918 errichtete Haus ist ein hervorragendes Beispiel für den spanischen Kolonialstil im Süden Kaliforniens. Es ist ein Teil eines größeren Besitzes, der später geteilt wurde. Im Laufe der Jahre wurde das Haus mehrfach umgebaut, bis die jetzigen Besitzer sich entschlossen, den ursprünglichen Charakter wiederherzustellen. Die Schönheit der Innenräume wird von den bei der Einrichtung verwendeten edlen Materialien besonders unterstrichen.

Dit huis is een uitstekend voorbeeld van de Spaanse koloniale stijl van het zuiden van Californië. Het is gebouwd tussen 1915 en 1918 en is een deel van het originele landhuis dat later is onderverdeeld. In de loop der jaren zijn er in de woning verschillende verbouwingen uitgevoerd, totdat de laatste eigenaren besloten om de originele geest in ere te herstellen. De elegante en nobele materialen die in de inrichting gebruikt zijn benadrukken de schoonheid van de interieurs.

Esta casa es una excelente muestra del estilo colonial español del sur de California; construida entre 1915 y 1918, es una parte de la finca original que fue posteriormente subdividida. A lo largo de los años, se realizaron diversas remodelaciones en la vivienda hasta que los últimos propietarios decidieron recuperar el espíritu original. Los elegantes y nobles materiales utilizados en la decoración acentúan la belleza de los interiores.

THE OBEROI VANYAVILÂS

© Oberoi Resorts

Nestling in the natural beauty of the wilds, The Oberoi Vanyavilâs is India's leading luxury jungle resort on the edge of the Ranthambore Tiger Reserve. The luxury tents with finely embroidered canopies, luxurious bathrooms and private walled gardens are in perfect contrast to the ruggedness of the jungle.

Niché dans la beauté sauvage de la nature, Oberoi Vanyavilâs est le principal hôtel de jungle de l'Inde, situé à la lisière de la Tiger reserve de Ranthambore. Les tentes luxueuses brodées de superbes voiles, les salles de bains de luxe et les jardins privés sont en parfait contraste avec l'aspérité de la jungle.

Protetto dalla bellezza di una natura incontaminata, The Oberoi Vanyavilâs è il più lussuoso jungle resort indiano, ubicato sul confine della Ranthambore Tiger Reserve. Le lussuose tende con letti a baldacchino finemente ricamati, bagni lussuosi e giardini privati protetti offrono un contrasto perfetto con il carattere assolutamente rustico della giungla.

Das Hotel The Oberoi Vanyavilâs, das inmitten der herrlichen wilden Natur errichtet wurde, ist Indiens führendes Luxus-Dschungelresort am Rande des Ranthambore-Tigerreservats. Die Luxuszelte mit bestickten Baldachinen, erlesenen Badezimmern und eigenen, ummauerten Gärten bilden einen interessanten Kontrast zum rauen Dschungel.

Verzonken in het natuurschoon van de wildernis, is Oberoi Vanyavilâs India's vooraanstaande luxe jungleresort aan de rand van het Tijgerreservaat Ranthambore. De luxe tenten met baldakijnen met fijn borduurwerk, luxe badkamers en ommuurde privé-tuinen vormen een perfect contrast met de woestheid van de jungle.

Enclavado en plena naturaleza salvaje, en los límites de la Reserva de Tigres de Ranthambore, The Oberoi Vanyavilâs es el principal complejo turístico de lujo en la selva de la India. Las espectaculares tiendas con baldaquines de elegantes bordados, cuartos de baño de lujo y jardines amurallados privados generan un contraste perfecto con la escabrosa jungla.

ANGSANA MALDIVES IHURU

Ho Kwoncjan/Architrave Design & Planning // © Angsana Media

The essence of Angsana is simple luxury and a fine spa on an idyllic island. Its eight luxurious double pavilions cover an extensive area behind the rooms. The rooms represent simple luxury, decorated with furniture and accessories that combine perfectly Asian style and a modern and contemporary touch.

Angsana ist der Inbegriff für schlichten Luxus und ein erlesenes Spa auf einer idyllischen Insel. Die acht luxuriösen Doppelpavillons erstrecken sich hinter den Zimmern über eine besonders ausgedehnte Fläche. Die Zimmer stehen für schlichten Luxus und sind mit Möbeln und Accessoires ausgestattet, die den asiatischen Stil mit einem modernen Touch versehen.

Luxe, sobriété et un superbe spa sur une île idyllique : voici l'essence d'Angsana. Ses huit pavillons doubles couvrent une vaste surface à l'arrière des chambres. Ces dernières sont décorées avec luxe et sobriété, à l'aide de meubles et d'accessoires associant parfaitement le style asiatique à une touche plus contemporaine.

De essentie van Angsana is luxe en een fijne spa op een idyllisch eiland. De acht luxueuze dubbele paviljoens nemen een grote ruimte achter de kamers in beslag. De kamers vertegenwoordigen luxe en zijn ingericht met meubels en accessoires die een Aziatische stijl perfect combineren met moderne en eigentijds trekjes.

L'essenza di Angsana è un lusso semplice e un bel centro benessere su un'isola idilliaca. Gli otto lussuosi doppi padiglioni si estendono su un'area molto ampia dietro le camere. Le camere offrono un lusso semplice e sono arricchite da mobili e accessori che combinano perfettamente lo stile asiatico con quello moderno e contemporaneo.

Angsana es un elegante y sencillo balneario de lujo ubicado en una isla idílica. Sus ocho lujosos pabellones dobles ocupan una amplia extensión tras las habitaciones. En estas se apuesta por el lujo austero, con una decoración a base de mobiliario y accesorios que combinan a la perfección con el estilo asiático, aquí aplicado con un toque moderno y contemporáneo.

RIAD VERT

Riad Vert/Isabel & Dominique Penot // www.riadvert.com // © Annakarin Quinto

Riad Vert is a small hotel offers its guests tranquility, relaxation and serenity. The interior circulation leads guests towards an old Moroccan palace, around charming interior and exterior spaces, oriental baths, and unique bedrooms, each with its own style.

Le Riad Vert est un petit hôtel qui offre à ses hôtes calme, détente et sérénité. Le parcours intérieur les mène vers un ancien palais marocain, entre salons intérieurs et extérieurs au charme fou, salles de bain orientales et chambres uniques, chacun ayant son style propre.

Il Riad Vert è un piccolo hotel che offre ai suoi clienti calma, relax e tranquillità. Il percorso interno guida gli ospiti in un antico palazzo marocchino, in mezzo a sale interne ed esterne piene d'incanto, a bagni orientali e a camere uniche, ognuna caratterizzata da uno stile proprio.

Riad Vert ist ein kleines Hotel, das seinen Gästen Ruhe, Entspannung und Gelassenheit bietet. Der Spaziergang durch das Gebäude führt die Gäste zu einem alten marrokanischen Palast, vorbei an zauberhaften Gemächern im Inneren und im Freien, orientalischen Bädern und einzigartigen Schlafgemächern, jedes von ihnen mit unterschiedlicher Einrichtung.

Riad Vert is een klein hotel dat de gasten rust, ontspanning en kalmte biedt. De gangen leiden de gasten naar een oud Marokkaans paleis, tussen betoverende binnen- en buitensalons, oriëntaalse badkamers en unieke kamers, elk met een eigen stijl.

Riad Vert es un pequeño hotel que ofrece a sus huéspedes calma, relajación y serenidad. El recorrido interior dirige a los huéspedes hacia un antiguo palacio marroquí, entre salones interiores y exteriores llenos de encanto, baños orientales y habitaciones únicas, cada una con su estilo propio.

AMANPURI

Edward Tuttle // designrealization@designrealization.net // © Amanresorts

Founded in 1988, Amanpuri, 'place of peace' in Sanskrit, was the first resort of the Aman chain. The hotel conveys the warmth and elegance of Thai culture through its architecture and décor while creating a perfect symbiosis with nature and transmitting the tranquillity to which its name alludes.

Amanpuri, „Ort des Friedens" auf Sanskrit wurde 1988 eröffnet und war das erste Resort der Hotelkette Aman. Das Hotel vermittelt die Wärme und Eleganz der Thai-Kultur durch seine Baukunst und Dekoration, die eine perfekte Symbiose mit der Natur bilden. Hierdurch wird die Ruhe vermittelt, für die der Hotelname Programm ist.

L'Amanpuri, « place de la paix » en sanskrit, a été inauguré en 1988 et représente le premier complexe hôtelier de la chaîne Aman. L'hôtel transmet la chaleur et l'élégance de la culture thaïlandaise à travers son architecture et sa décoration, parvenant à une symbiose parfaite avec la nature et dégageant la tranquillité caractéristique de son nom.

Amanpuri, "plaats van vrede" in het Sanskriet, werd in 1988 officieel in gebruik genomen en is het eerste resort van de hotelketen Aman. Het hotel straalt dankzij de architectuur en inrichting de warmte en elegantie van de Thaise cultuur uit, waarbij men erin is geslaagd om een perfecte symbiose met de natuur te verkrijgen en de rust die de naam al aangeeft wordt uitgedragen.

L'Amanpuri, «luogo di pace» in sanscrito, è stato inaugurato nel 1988 ed è il primo resort della catena Aman. L'hotel trasmette il calore e l'eleganza della cultura tailandese tramite gli elementi architettonici e le decorazioni, ottenendo una perfetta simbiosi con la natura e trasmettendo così la tranquillità che rievoca il nome stesso della struttura.

Amanpuri, «lugar de la paz» en sánscrito, fue inaugurado en 1988 y es el primer hotel de la cadena Aman. El lugar transmite la calidez y la elegancia de la cultura tailandesa a través de su arquitectura y decoración, logrando una perfecta simbiosis con la naturaleza y transmitiendo así la tranquilidad que su nombre indica.

DWARIKA'S HOTEL

Dwarika Das Shrestha // © Dwarika Hotel

Built upon a rich tradition of Nepali hospitality and incorporating some of the country's most exquisite architectural traditions, this hotel is an authentic experience of Nepal's ancient cultural heritage. The hotel houses a collection of artefacts from the 13th century onwards, and the buildings and courtyards house some of Nepal's best craftsmanship.

Fondé sur une longue tradition d'hospitalité népalaise et mettant en scène certains des meilleurs principes architecturaux du pays, cet hôtel est un exemple authentique de l'héritage culturel du Népal. L'hôtel héberge une collection d'objets d'art datant pour les plus anciens du XIIIe siècle et les différents édifices, de même que les cours, comportent certaines des plus belles pièces d'artisanat du Népal.

Frutto della ricca storia di ospitalità nepalese, questo hotel coniuga alcune delle più squisite tradizioni architettoniche del paese consentendo di avvicinarsi in modo autentico all'antica eredità culturale del Nepal. L'hotel ospita una collezione di opere a partire dal XIII secolo mentre gli edifici e i cortili mostrano le migliori lavorazioni artigianali del Nepal.

Dieses Hotel, das auf der berühmten nepalesischen Gastfreundschaft aufbaut und einige der beeindruckendsten architektonischen Traditionen des Landes in sich trägt, lässt die Gäste das enorme kulturelle Erbe Nepals erleben. Das Hotel beherbergt eine Sammlung von Artefakten aus der Zeit ab dem 13. Jahrhundert, und die Gebäude und Höfe sind Beispiele bester nepalesischer Handwerkskunst.

Dit hotel is gebouwd op basis van een rijke traditie van Nepalese gastvrijheid en heeft enkele van de beste bouwtradities van het land, waarmee het een authentieke ervaring van de oude culturele erfenis van Nepal is. Het hotel herbergt een collectie kunstwerken vanaf de 13de eeuw en de gebouwen en binnenplaatsen laten voorbeelden van het beste vakmanschap van Nepal zien.

Este hotel, fruto de la legendaria hospitalidad nepalí, adopta algunas de las tradiciones arquitectónicas más exquisitas del país y ofrece una experiencia auténtica del legado cultural ancestral del Nepal. El hotel alberga una colección de objetos del siglo XIII en adelante, y los edificios y patios acogen algunas de las mejores artesanías nepalís.

HOUSE **IN IBIZA**

Víctor Espósito (Owner) / © S. Dos Santos/Inside/Cover

This rural house is characterized by the island's own architectural style. Inside, the furniture and the modern sculptural pieces combine with old restored items such as amphorae, fireplaces or dressers. The ceiling has been preserved along with some of the walls from the original construction in order to accentuate the traditional style of this home.

Cette maison rurale affiche le style architectural typique de l'île. A l'intérieur, le mobilier et les sculptures modernes se mêlent à d'anciens vestiges restaurés, comme les amphores, cheminées ou armoires. Le toit et certains murs de la construction originale ont été préservés pour accentuer le style traditionnel de la demeure.

Lo stile architettonico di questo agroturismo di Ibiza è tipico dell'isola. Dentro, i mobili e le sculture moderne si fondono con oggetti antichi restaurati, come anfore, camini e armadi. I soffitti e alcune delle pareti originali sono state conservate per sottolineare lo stile tradizionale della residenza.

Dieses Landhotel zeichnet sich durch die für die Insel typische Bauweise aus. Im Inneren mischen sich moderne Möbel und Skulpturen mit restaurierten antiken Sammelstücken, wie Amphoren, offene Kamine und Schränke. Das Dach und einige Wände des Originalbaus wurden beibehalten, um den traditionellen Stil des Hauses zu betonen.

Dit huis op het platteland kenmerkt zich doordat het blijk geeft van de typische bouwstijl van het eiland. In het interieur zijn het meubilair en de moderne beeldhouwwerken gecombineerd met oude gerestaureerde voorwerpen, zoals amfora's, open haarden of kasten. De plafonds en enkele muren van de originele constructie zijn bewaard gebleven om de traditionele stijl van de woning te benadrukken.

Esta casa rural se caracteriza por presentar el estilo arquitectónico propio de la isla. En el interior, muebles y esculturas modernos se mezclan con antiguos objetos restaurados, como ánforas, chimeneas o armarios. Se preservaron el techo y algunas de las paredes de la construcción original para acentuar el estilo tradicional de la vivienda.

PURO HOTEL

Alvaro Planchuelo // www.alvaroplanchuelo.com // © Puro Hotel

Situated in the old town of Palma de Mallorca, this hotel is the result of the remodelling of an ancient palatial house with styles dating back from the fourteenth to the eighteenth centuries. The timber, the stone and the handcrafted ornaments – such as feather screens and cushions made from Indian saris – give the hotel a Bohemian touch.

Cet hôtel est le résultat de la rénovation d'un ancien palais, dont les styles s'étendent du XIVe au XVIIIe siècle, situé dans le centre historique de Palma de Majorque. Le bois, la pierre et les éléments décoratifs faits main, comme les abat-jour en plumes et les coussins de saris indiens, apportent à l'hôtel une touche de bohême.

Questo hotel è il risultato della ristrutturazione di un antico palazzo situato nel centro storico di Palma di Maiorca il cui stile abbraccia un periodo che va dal XIV al XVIII secolo. Il legno, la pietra e gli elementi decorativi realizzati artigianalmente come i paralumi di piume e i cuscini di sari indiano, danno all'hotel un tocco bohémien.

Dieses Hotel ist das Resultat der Renovierung eines alten Palastes, dessen Baustile vom 14. bis zum 18. Jahrhundert reichen und der sich im alten Stadtkern von Palma de Mallorca befindet. Holz, Stein und handgefertigte Dekorelemente wie Wandschirme aus Federn und Kissen aus indischen Saris verleihen dem Hotel seine künstlerische Note.

Dit hotel is het resultaat van een renovatie van een voormalig paleis, gebouwd in verschillende stijlen uit de 14de tot de 18de eeuw, gelegen in de oude binnenstad van Palma de Mallorca. Hout, steen en handgemaakte decoratieve elementen zoals lampenkappen met veren en kussens van Indische sari's geven het hotel een Boheems tintje.

Este hotel es el resultado de la remodelación de un antiguo palacio, cuyos estilos abarcan desde el siglo XIV al XVIII, situado en el casco antiguo de Palma de Mallorca. La madera, la piedra y elementos decorativos hechos a mano, como pantallas de plumas y cojines de saris indios, dan al hotel un toque bohemio.

Type plan

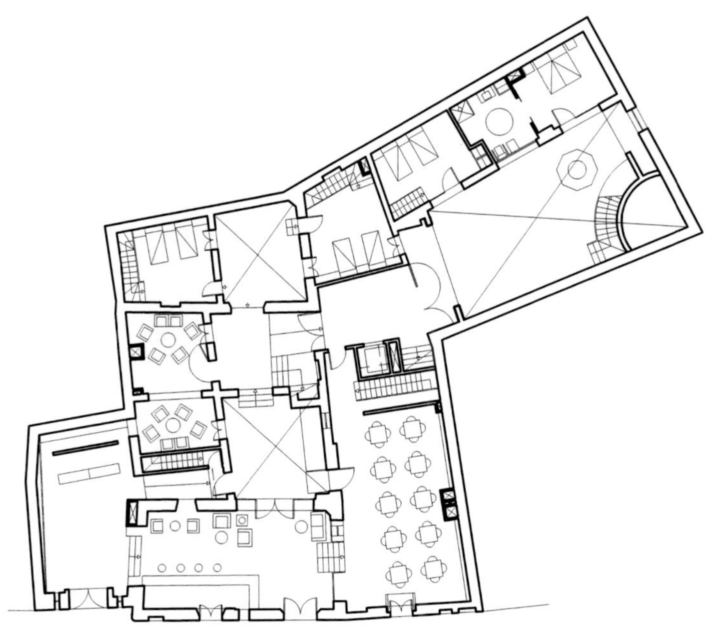

Ground floor

RED CAPITAL CLUB

Laurence J. Brahm/Red Capital Club // www.redcapitalclub.com.cn // © Minoru Iwasaki

Dedicated to China's burgeoning "red capitalists" this club is hidden in an ancient hutong alleyway located near the courtyard homes of many of China's leaders. The lounge cigar divan is like stepping into Mao's private meeting room. The furnishings were originally used by the government in the 1950s. Who knows, maybe he is listening.

Entièrement dédié au « capitalisme rouge », florissant en Chine, ce club se cache dans une ancienne ruelle *hutong* située à proximité des maisons à cour de nombreux dirigeants chinois. Le salon à cigares donne l'impression de se trouver dans une salle de réunion privée de Mao. Les meubles étaient à l'origine utilisés par le gouvernement dans les années 1950... Peut-être que quelqu'un nous écoute, qui sait ?

Dedicato ai «capitalisti rossi», nuovi borghesi cinesi, questo club è nascosto in un vecchio vicolo hutong vicino alle case tradizionali dotate di cortile interno possedute da numerosi leader cinesi. Il divano da sigaro ci proietta nella stanza che Mao utilizzava per gli incontri privati. Gli arredi sono stati originariamente utilizzati dal governo negli anni '50. Chissà... magari ci sta ascoltando.

Dieser Club, der den „roten Kapitalisten" gewidmet ist, befindet sich in einer versteckten Hutong-Gasse in der Nähe der Wohnhöfe, in denen zahlreiche chinesische Führungspersönlichkeiten zu Hause sind. Der Diwan in der Lounge wirkt, als ob man direkt in Maos privates Besprechungszimmer eingetreten sei. Die Möbel wurden in den fünfziger Jahren von der chinesischen Regierung benutzt. Und wer weiß... vielleicht wohnt in ihnen sogar noch Maos Geist.

Deze club, gewijd aan China's opgekomen "rode kapitalisten" ligt verscholen in een oud hutong steegje, vlakbij de huizen met binnenhoven van vele van China's leiders. Door de *cigar divan* in de lounge lijkt het alsof u Mao's privé-vergaderzaal binnenstapt. De meubels werden oorspronkelijk gebruikt door de regering in de jaren '50. Wie weet, misschien luistert hij wel.

Dedicado a los florecientes «capitalistas rojos» de China, este club se encuentra oculto en un antiguo callejón *hutong* situado cerca de las mansiones con patio interior de muchos dirigentes chinos. Al internarse en el salón de fumadores se tiene la sensación de estar adentrándose en la sala de reuniones privada de Mao. El mobiliario perteneció originalmente al Gobierno de la década de 1950, así que ¿quién sabe?, quizá el líder esté escuchando.

NOCTILUCA

Renee Armas // rearmas@hotmail.com // © Virginia del Giudice

Immediately on passing the exterior wall, a carved wooden door from Thailand opens to numerous courtyards and galleries designed for relaxation. Exoticism defines the eclectic character of the interior design, which boasts furniture made of wood and natural fibers, white cotton fabrics and oriental rugs.

Juste après avoir franchi un mur extérieur, une porte en bois sculpté originaire de Thaïlande, s'ouvre sur de nombreux patios et galeries. L'exotisme marque le design d'intérieur au caractère éclectique d'où se détachent des meubles en bois et fibre naturelle, des tissus en coton blanc et tapis orientaux.

Appena varcato il muro esterno, una porta di legno intagliata, originaria della Tailandia, si apre su numerosi cortili e gallerie concepiti per il riposo. L'esotismo definisce il design degli interni, dal carattere eclettico e dove spiccano i mobili di legno e fibra naturale, i tessuti di color bianco cotone e i tappeti orientali.

Hinter der Außenmauer befindet sich eine typisch thailändische Eingangstür aus geschnitztem Holz, durch die man in die zahlreichen Innenhöfe und Loggien gelangt, die zum Erholen und Entspannen einladen. Als Wesensmerkmal der Inneneinrichtung ist ihre exotische Stilmischung hervorzuheben: Holzmöbel, Naturfasern und weiße Baumwolltextilien werden mit orientalischen Teppichen kombiniert.

Direct nadat men door de buitenmuur naar binnen gaat, opent een deur met houtsnijwerk, afkomstig uit Thailand de toegang naar de patio's en veranda's die zijn ontworpen om uit te rusten. Het interieurontwerp wordt gekenmerkt door zijn exotische karakter met een eclectisch tintje, waarin houten en natuurvezel meubels, witte katoenen stoffen en oriëntaalse tapijten opvallen.

Apenas se atraviesa el muro exterior, una puerta de madera tallada procedente de Tailandia se abre a patios y galerías concebidos para el descanso. El exotismo define el diseño del interior, de carácter ecléctico y en el que destacan los muebles de madera y fibra natural, los tejidos de color blanco algodón y las alfombras orientales.

BED

Oliver & Pascale Hoyos // © Pep Escoda

The principle behind the design of BED was to create a comfortable and intimate atmosphere that reflects a hedonistic culture. The decorative details, as well as the technical elements implemented in the project's design, complement the beds' strong presence, creating a special ambience.

À l'origine du design de BED était la volonté de créer une atmosphère intime et agréable qui reflèterait les principes de l'hédonisme. Les détails de la décoration, de même que les éléments techniques mis en place pour la conception du projet, viennent ajouter à la prestance du BED et lui confèrent une atmosphère particulière.

Il principio alla base del progetto BED era creare un'atmosfera confortevole e intima che riflettesse una cultura edonistica. I dettagli decorativi, oltre agli elementi tecnici implementati nel design del progetto, integrano la forte presenza dei letti, creando un'atmosfera speciale.

Das Design von BED stützte sich auf die Leitlinie, eine komfortable und intime Atmosphäre zu schaffen, die eine hedonistische Kultur widerspiegelt. Die dekorativen Details sowie die technischen Elemente dieses Projekts unterstreichen die starke Präsenz und schaffen ein ganz besonderes Ambiente.

Het principe achter het ontwerp van BED was om een comfortabele en intieme entourage te creëren, waarin een hedonistische cultuur weerspiegeld wordt. De decoratieve details, evenals de technische elementen die in het projectontwerp zijn geïmplementeerd, maken de sterke aanwezigheid van het bed compleet, waardoor een speciale sfeer ontstaat.

El objetivo del diseño de BED era crear un ambiente cómodo e íntimo, símbolo de una cultura hedonista. Los detalles decorativos, como los elementos técnicos incorporados al diseño del proyecto, complementan la contundente presencia de las camas y, en conjunto, generan un ambiente singular.

MAYA UBUD BALINESE VILLA

Denton Corker Marshall // www.dentoncorkermarshall.com // © Denton Corker Marshall

Maya Ubud juggles with the new and the traditional in every part of its design. Its architecture is sustainable, with bamboo, thatched *alang-alang* roofs, and soft river stone as their main components. Bali's culture and heritage are celebrated in every nook and cranny.

Maya Ubud jongle avec les concepts, comme l'ancien et le nouveau, dans tout son design. L'architecture est viable, bambou, toit chaumé d'*alang-alang* et pierres lisses de rivières étant les composants essentiels. La culture et l'héritage balinais sont célébrés en tout point.

Il progetto di Maya Ubud gioca costantemente con i concetti di innovazione e tradizione. Con un'architettura sostenibile, utilizzando il bambù, pietra morbida di fiume e tetti di paglia tipo *alang-alang* come elementi principali, il patrimonio culturale di Bali emerge in ogni aspetto.

Das Design von Maya Ubud jongliert mit traditionellen und modernen Konzepten. Die Architektur beruft sich auf traditionelle Materialien, wie vor allem Bambus, Strohdächer im alang-alang-Stil und weicher Flussstein. Balinesische Kultur und Tradition zeigen sich hier in jedem Winkel.

In het ontwerp van Maya Ubud wordt constant gespeeld met de concepten van het nieuwe en het traditionele. Met een duurzame architectuur, waarin bamboe, zachte riviersteen en rieten daken van het type "alang-alang" gebruikt zijn als belangrijkste elementen, is het culturele erfgoed van het eiland overal aanwezig.

El diseño de Maya Ubud juega constantemente con los conceptos de lo nuevo y lo tradicional. Con una arquitectura sostenible, utilizando el bambú, cantos rodados y techos de paja tipo *alang-alang* como elementos principales, en todos los rincones se celebra el patrimonio cultural de la isla de Bali.

HOUSE IN **HONDA**

Guillermo Arias + Luis Cuartas // www.octubre.com.co // © Eduardo Consuegra

This dwelling comprises two properties facing the street, that once featured residential and storage buildings. Only the façades and colonial stone walls of these buildings were preserved and incorporated into the project. A labyrinth-like layout organizes a multitude of spaces for relaxing and contemplating the landscape.

Cette habitation comporte deux propriétés donnant sur la rue ; il s'agissait autrefois d'un immeuble résidentiel et d'un entrepôt. Ce projet n'a préservé que leurs façades et leurs murs en pierre de style colonial. L'agencement en labyrinthe des bâtiments a permis d'organiser de nombreux espaces de détente offrant de superbes vues sur le paysage.

Questa struttura comprende due proprietà affacciate sulla strada, un tempo edifici residenziali e magazzini. Solo le facciate e le pareti in pietra coloniale sono state conservate e inserite nel progetto. Una struttura labirintica accoglie molteplici spazi dedicati al relax e alla contemplazione del paesaggio.

Diese Wohnung erstreckt sich über zwei Immobilien, die zur Straße hin gelegen sind und einst Wohn- und Lagerräume beherbergten. Nur die Fassaden und die kolonialen Steinmauern dieser Gebäude wurden erhalten und in das Projekt integriert. Die labyrinth-ähnliche Raumaufteilung schafft viele unterschiedliche Bereiche, die sich zum Entspannen und Beobachten der umgebenden Landschaft anbieten.

Deze woning is opgebouwd uit twee panden met de gevel aan de straatkant, die eens prominente woon- en opslagruimtes waren. Alleen de gevels en de koloniale stenen muren van deze gebouwen zijn behouden gebleven en in het project opgenomen. Een doolhofachtige vormgeving omvat een groot aantal vertrekken om te ontspannen en het landschap te aanschouwen.

Esta vivienda engloba dos propiedades orientadas a la calle, las cuales acogieron otrora edificios residenciales y almacenes. Únicamente las fachadas y las tapias coloniales de los edificios antiguos se han conservado e incorporado al proyecto. Los múltiples espacios están organizados en una disposición laberíntica que propicia el relax y la contemplación del paisaje.

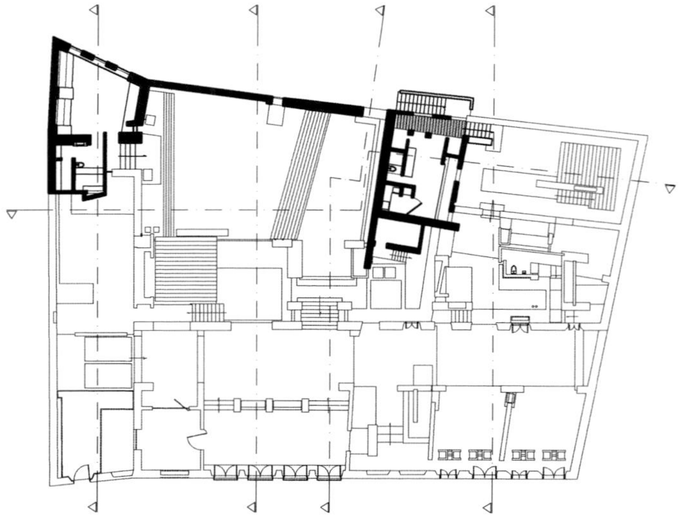

Ground floor

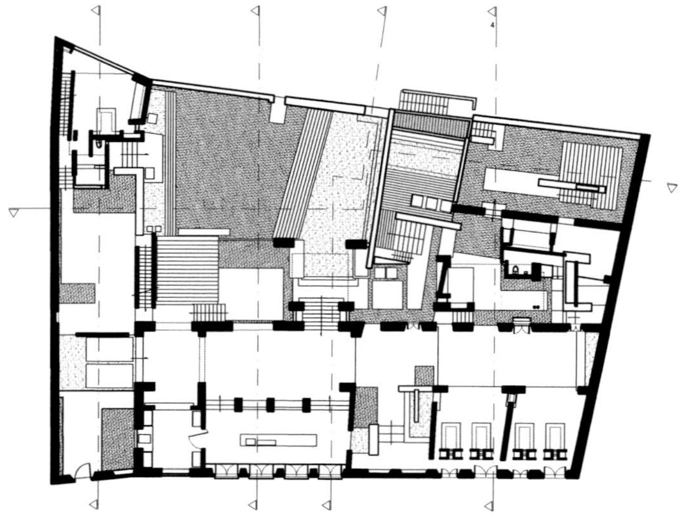

Second floor

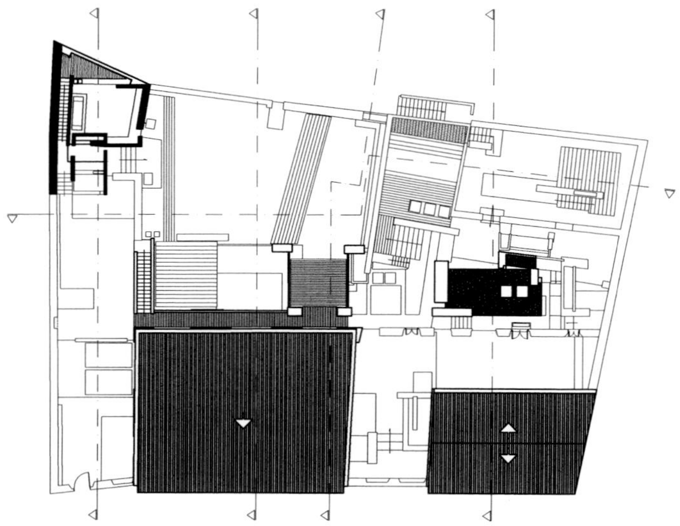

Roof plan

ASIA DE CUBA

Melissa Castañeda de León de Peralta // melissa@asiadecubaperu.com // © José Gamboa

Asia de Cuba was designed in response to two distinct ideas that, visually, imply clearly differentiated aesthetics. The restaurant's inclusion of ornamentation representative of Oriental cultures within a space of eminently Occidental forms and materials breaks with the traditional aesthetic of a space.

La conception d'Asia de Cuba répond à deux idées différentes donnant naissance à deux esthétiques bien distinctes sur le plan visuel. Dans ce restaurant, l'inclusion d'une décoration propre aux cultures orientales dans un espace essentiellement consacré aux formes et matériaux occidentaux permet de rompre avec l'esthétique traditionnelle des lieux.

Asia de Cuba nasce per rispondere a due diverse idee che, visivamente, implicano un'estetica chiaramente differenziata. L'inserimento nel ristorante di elementi decorativi rappresentativi delle culture orientali all'interno di uno spazio caratterizzato prevalentemente da forme e materiali occidentali rompe con l'estetica tradizionale.

Asia de Cuba wurde als Antwort auf zwei verschiedene Ideen entworfen, die eine äußerst unterschiedlich Ästhetik aufweisen. Da im Restaurant typische Dekoelemente aus den asiatischen Kulturen in Räumen eingesetzt wurden, die von westlichen Formen und Materialien beherrscht werden, wurde mit der herkömmlichen Raumwirkung gebrochen.

Asia de Cuba is ontworpen in overeenstemming met twee verschillende ideeën die zich visueel gezien duidelijk van elkaar onderscheiden qua esthetiek. De inrichting van het restaurant, met versieringen die kenmerkend zijn voor de oosterse culturen, binnen een ruimte met verheven vormen en materialen, breekt met de traditionele esthetica.

Asia de Cuba se diseñó en respuesta a dos ideas distintas que, en términos visuales, implican estéticas claramente diferenciadas. La inclusión en el restaurante de ornamentación representativa de las culturas orientales en el seno de un espacio de formas y materiales eminentemente occidentales rompe con la estética tradicional del espacio.

RED CAPITAL RANCH

Laurence J. Brahm/Red Capital Club // www.redcapitalclub.com.cn // © Minoru Iwasaki

This resort is a rustic and rambling collection of ten ancient restored luxury Chinese villas, a traditional teahouse and a Tibetan spa. The area was once the hunting grounds of Qing emperors, and the hunting-lodge interiors of the Ranch evoke Manchurian history, with intriguing antiques and artefacts from China and Tibet in every room.

Cet hôtel consiste en une collection rustique et hétérogène comprenant de luxueuses villas chinoises restaurées, une maison de thé traditionnelle et un spa tibétain. Cet endroit était autrefois le terrain de chasse des empereurs de la dynastie Qing. L'intérieur du Ranch, aux allures de pavillon de chasse, reflète l'histoire de la Manchourie avec, dans chaque chambre, des antiquités et œuvres d'art intrigantes provenant de la Chine et du Tibet.

Questo resort è una collezione rustica e irregolare di dieci antiche ville cinesi di lusso restaurate, una casa da tè tradizionale e un centro benessere tibetano. L'area era un tempo zona di caccia degli imperatori Qing e gli interni del rifugio della tenuta rievocano la storia della Manciuria con affascinanti pezzi antichi e artefatti cinesi e tibetani esposti in ogni stanza.

Dieses rustikal anmutende Resort umfasst zehn restaurierte chinesische Luxus-Villen, ein traditionelles Teehaus und ein tibetanisches Spa auf den ehemaligen Jagdgründen der Kaiser der Qing-Dynastie. Die Inneneinrichtung im Stile von Jagdhütten lässt die Geschichte der Mandschurei aufleben und jedes einzelne Zimmer besticht durch herrliche Antiquitäten und Artefakte aus China und Tibet.

Dit resort bestaat uit een landelijke en breedvoerige collectie van tien oude, gerenoveerde luxe Chinese villa's, een traditioneel theehuis en een Tibetaanse spa. Het grondgebied omvatte ooit de jachtgronden van de Qing keizers en de interieurs van de jachtverblijven van de ranch brengen de geschiedenis van Mantsjoerije in herinnering, met intrigerend antiek en kunstvoorwerpen uit China en Tibet in elke kamer.

Este centro vacacional es un conjunto rústico y laberíntico de diez antiguas y lujosas mansiones chinas restauradas, una casa de té tradicional y un balneario tibetano. La zona ocupó antaño los terrenos de caza de los emperadores Qing. Los interiores del pabellón de caza de la hacienda evocan la historia de Manchuria, con enigmáticas antigüedades y objetos chinos y tibetanos en cada estancia.

DAR LES CIGOGNES

Charles Boccara // © Dar Les Cigognes

This traditional Moroccan house, built during the seventeenth century, once belonged to a merchant who did business with the nearby royal palace of Marrakech. The furniture and decorative items –among which the carved wood doors, hammered silver mirrors, and bronze lamps are exceptional– are locally produced.

Dieses traditionelle marokkanische Haus aus dem 17. Jahrhundert gehörte früher einem Kaufmann, der mit dem benachbarten Königspalast in Marrakesch Geschäfte machte. Mobiliar und Dekor, die insbesondere durch die geschnitzten Holztüren, die silbernen Spiegel mit Hammerschlag-Verzierung und die bronzenen Lampen bestechen, wurden vor Ort angefertigt.

Cette maison marocaine traditionnelle, construite au cours du XVIIe siècle, appartenait autrefois à un marchand qui faisait du commerce avec le palais royal de Marrakech, situé à proximité. Le mobilier et les objets décoratifs sont issus de l'artisanat local ; on distingue notamment les portes en bois sculpté, les miroirs en argent martelé et les lampes en bronze.

Dit traditionele Marokkaanse huis, gebouwd in de 17de eeuw, behoorde indertijd toe aan een handelsman die zaken deed met het nabijgelegen koninklijk paleis van Marrakech. Het meubilair en de decoratieve voorwerpen– waaronder het houtsnijwerk, de spiegels van gehamerd zilveren en bronzen lampen opvallen– zijn van plaatselijke fabricage.

Questa casa tradizionale marocchina, costruita nel XVII secolo, è appartenuta a un mercante che commerciava con il vicino palazzo reale di Marrakech. Mobili e arredi - tra cui si impongono le porte in legno intagliato, gli specchi d'argento battuto e i lampadari in bronzo - sono di manifattura locale.

Esta casa tradicional marroquí, construida en el siglo XVII, perteneció en su día a un mercader que negociaba con el vecino palacio real de Marrakech. El mobiliario y los objetos decorativos –entre los que destacan las puertas de madera tallada, los espejos de plata martillada y las lámparas de bronce– son de manufactura local.

The Orientalist Poster

MANDARIN ORIENTAL DHARA DHEVI

Nadadhorn Dhamabutra, Rachen Intawong // © Mandarin Oriental Dhara Dhevi, Chiang Mai

Mandarin Oriental Dhara Dhevi is a living museum, where traditional Lanna culture merges with the splendor of the Asian colonial period to create a sophisticated and harmonious atmosphere. The design of the pavilions is influenced by the indigenous architectural style, with sloping tile roofs and an abundance of local teak woodwork.

Das Hotel Mandarin Oriental Dhara Dhevi ist ein lebendiges Museum, in dem die traditionelle Lanna-Kultur und der Glanz der asiatischen Kolonialzeit vereint wurden, um ein harmonisch wirkendes, exquisites Ambiente zu schaffen. Das Design der Pavillons wurde vom traditionellen einheimischen Baustil inspiriert, der sich durch die typischen schrägen Ziegeldächer und den Einsatz von Teakholz aus der Region auszeichnet.

Mandarin Oriental Dhara Dhevi est un musée vivant, un endroit où la culture traditionnelle Lanna et la splendeur coloniale asiatique se rencontrent pour donner naissance à une atmosphère harmonieuse et sophistiquée. Le design des pavillons s'inspire du style architectural autochtone, avec des toitures inclinées en tuiles et la prédominance du bois de tec, propre à la région.

Mandarin Oriental Dhara Dhevi bouwt een levendig museum, een plaats waar de traditionele Lannacultuur en alle Aziatische koloniale pracht worden verenigd om een verfijnde en harmonieuze sfeer te scheppen. Het ontwerp van de paviljoens is beïnvloed door de autochtone bouwstijl, met schuine daken met dakpannen en gebruik op grote schaal van teakhout uit de regio.

Mandarin Oriental Dhara Dhevi è un museo vivente, un luogo in cui la cultura tradizionale Lanna e lo splendore coloniale asiatico si fondono per creare un ambiente sofisticato e armonioso. Il progetto dei padiglioni è influenzato dallo stile architettonico locale, con i tipici tetti inclinati di tegole e l'uso massiccio di legno di teak, tipico della regione.

Mandarin Oriental Dhara Dhevi constituye un museo vivo, un lugar donde la cultura tradicional Lanna y el esplendor colonial asiático se unen para crear un ambiente sofisticado y armonioso. El diseño de los pabellones está influenciado por el estilo arquitectónico autóctono, con sus inclinadas cubiertas de tejas y el uso extensivo de madera de teca, propia de la región.

NOMADS

Concrete Architectural Associates // www.concreteamsterdam.nl // © Concrete Architectural Associates

Different types of lighting are used in the design. In the restaurant, handmade Moroccan lampshades provide a diffuse, mystic lighting. Nomads' color range–reds, browns and golden tones–is inspired by *One Thousand and One Nights*, producing an Arabian-Nights-like, mystic, Oriental feel. A poem written in Arabic covers the mirrors along the outside walls.

Des abat-jour marocains faits main ont été installés dans les différentes parties du restaurant afin de générer un éclairage diffus et mystique. La gamme de couleurs du Nomads est inspirée du recueil de contes *Les Mille et Une Nuits*, le tout arborant l'aspect des nuits d'Arabie et du mysticisme oriental : rouges, marrons et dorés. Les murs, sur lesquels un poème arabe a été écrit, sont recouverts de miroirs.

Nelle varie aree del ristorante sono stati inseriti dei portalampade marocchini lavorati a mano, che creano un'illuminazione sfumata e mistica. La gamma di colori del Nomads si ispira alle *Mille e una notte*, ogni cosa richiama le notti d'Arabia e la mistica orientale: rossi, marroni e oro. Le pareti sono ricoperte di specchi, sui quali è stato trascritto un poema in arabo.

In den einzelnen Abteilen des Restaurants wurden handgefertigte marokkanische Lampen angebracht, die für eine diffuse und mystische Beleuchtung sorgen. Die Farbpalette des Nomads wurde von den Erzählungen *1001 Nacht* inspiriert: die Räume, in denen Rot-, Braun- und Goldtöne dominieren, strahlen die Atmosphäre arabischer Nächte und orientalischer Mystik aus. Die Wände sind mit Spiegeln geschmückt, die arabische Poesie ziert.

In de verschillende afdelingen van het restaurant zijn met de hand vervaardigde Marokkaanse lamphouders geïnstalleerd, die diffuus en mystiek licht verspreiden. Het kleurengamma van Nomads is geïnspireerd op de vertellingen uit *Duizend-en-één-nacht*; de nachten van Arabië en de oriëntaalse mystiek worden in herinnering gebracht in rode, bruine en gouden kleuren. De muren zijn bedekt met spiegels, waarop een gedicht in het Arabisch is geschreven.

En los diferentes apartados del restaurante se instalaron portalámparas marroquíes elaborados a mano que crean una iluminación difusa y mística. La gama de colores del Nomads está inspirada en los cuentos de *Las mil y una noches*, todo tiene el aspecto de las noches de Arabia y de la mística oriental: rojos, marrones y dorados. Las paredes se encuentran recubiertas de espejos, donde se ha escrito un poema en árabe.

BAISHAYUAN TEA HOUSE

Alan Chan Design Company // www.alanchandesign.com // © Alvin Chan

The architecture of this tea house is based on the design of traditional Suzhou Gardens with the building outline preserved for keeping the cultural uniqueness of the local city. Inside the building, there is a thorough constructional change of the interior to achieve a new contemporary look for serving high-profile customers.

L'architecture de cette maison de thé s'inspire du design des jardins traditionnels de Suzhou, avec une silhouette conçue pour préserver la singularité culturelle de la ville. À l'intérieur, un profond changement structurel a été effectué afin d'obtenir un nouvel aspect contemporain visant à accueillir une clientèle de renom.

L'architettura di questa casa da tè si basa sul modello dei tradizionali giardini Suzhou con il profilo dell'edificio ben preservato al fine di conservare l'unicità culturale della cittadina. All'interno è stato fatto un accurato lavoro di ristrutturazione per ottenere un look contemporaneo e soddisfare le necessità di clienti di alto profilo.

Der Entwurf dieses Teehauses basiert auf der Bauform der traditionellen Gärten von Suzhou. Die äußeren Begrenzungen des Gebäudes wurden erhalten, um die kulturelle Einzigartigkeit der Stadt zu bewahren. Im Inneren des Gebäudes wurden erhebliche bauliche Veränderungen vorgenommen, um einen zeitgenössischen Look zu kreieren, der anspruchsvolle Kunden ansprechen soll.

De architectuur van dit theehuis is gebaseerd op het ontwerp van traditionele Suzhou tuinen, waarbij de contour van het gebouw bewaard is gebleven, om de culturele uniekheid van de plaats in stand te houden. Het gebouw heeft van binnen een diepgaande constructieve verandering ondergaan om een nieuwe eigentijdse look te verkrijgen, ten dienste van de vooraanstaande klanten.

La arquitectura de esta casa de té se basa en el diseño de los jardines tradicionales de Suzhou. Mientras que el contorno del edificio se ha conservado para mantener la unicidad cultural de la ciudad, el interior se ha sometido a una remodelación integral en aras de ofrecer a su prominente clientela una ambientación más contemporánea.

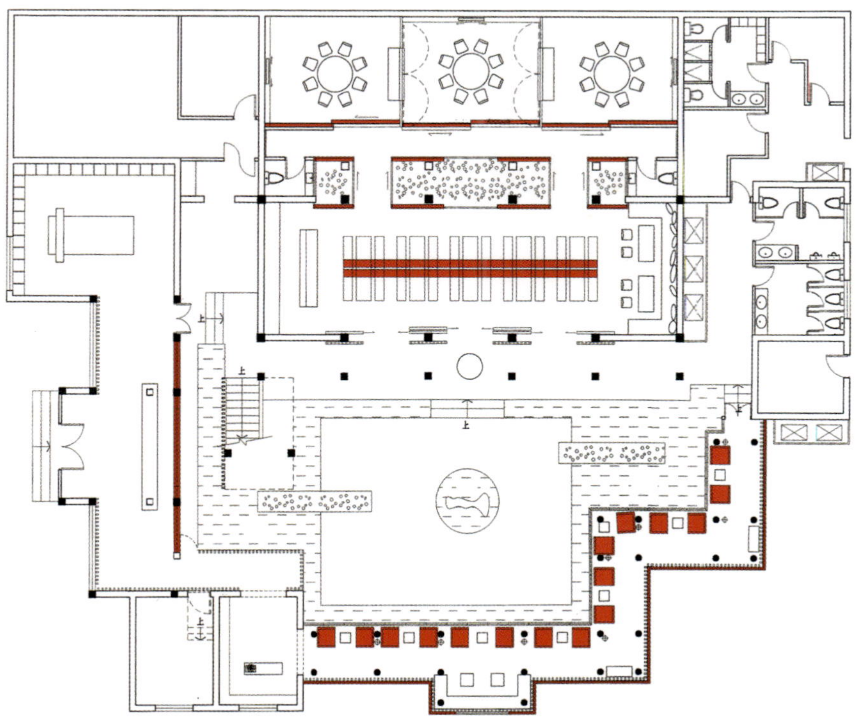

Floor plan

KAMATH HOUSE

Revathi & Vasant Kamath // © Ram Rahman

The Kamath House is an attempt to heal the wounds inflicted on the earth and establish a niche in the eco-system by regenerating the vegetation and creating a space and visual style based on the rearrangement of materials found on the grounds, on architecture that celebrates and nurtures the characteristics of natural elements. This project embodies a lifestyle in which the human patterns within nature are constantly evolving.

Kamath's House est une tentative pour guérir la terre et nicher un écosystème susceptible de régénérer la forêt sur le site et pour laquelle l'architecture est une redistribution de matériaux, ça et là, pour créer espace et esthétisme. Une architecture selon laquelle les qualités vitales des éléments sont célébrées et nourries. Kamath House est un espace où l'évolution continue des modèles humains au sein de la nature est devenu un mode de vie.

Kamath House tenta di sanare le ferite della terra e definire una piccola zona nell'ecosistema che rigeneri il verde e crei spazio ed estetica modificando i materiali utilizzati nel progetto e intorno a questo. Si tratta di uno spazio rappresentativo di uno stile di vita in cui il modello umano all'interno della natura è in continua evoluzione.

Mit Kamath's House wird versucht, die offenen Wunden zu heilen und eine Nische im Öko-System zu errichten, in der sich das Grün ringsherum regenerieren kann. Architektur bedeutet hier das Erschaffen von Raum und Ästethik durch eine Neubearbeitung der sich auf und um das Baugelände herum befindlichen Materialien, und auch, die Natur zu achten und zu bewahren. Dieses projekt repräsentiert einen Ort, in dem sich die menschliche Lebensweise innerhalb der Natur stetig entwickelt.

Kamath House tracht om de wonden van de grond te helen en een kleine zone in het ecosysteem in te richten waarin het groen wordt hersteld en ruimte en esthetica worden gecreëerd door het gebruik van alternatieve materialen op en rond het terrein. Dit project is een representatieve ruimte van een levensstijl waarin het menselijke model binnen de natuur voortdurend in ontwikkeling is.

Kamath House trata de cicatrizar las heridas de la tierra y establecer una pequeña zona en el ecosistema que regenere verde y cree espacio y estética mediante un cambio de los materiales usados en y alrededor del solar. Este proyecto es un espacio representativo de un estilo de vida en donde el modelo humano dentro de la naturaleza está en continua evolución.

JAPANESE STYLE

VILLA **SALINA**

Prima Design // www.primadesign.it // © Giorgio Baroni

This attractive villa dates back to the year 1700 and was originally a malvasia wine-producing farm. Its restoration aimed to preserve the local architectural style and at the same time, add a modern air. The white color enhances the purity of the lines and the decoration creates delicate and luminous rooms adorned with ethnic rugs and Arabic decorative objects.

Cette belle villa, datant de 1700, était à l'origine une ferme ou l'on fabriquait le vin de malvoisie. La restauration devait garder l'esprit de l'architecture de la région et apporter, en même temps, une touche moderne. Le blanc exalte la pureté des lignes et la décoration crée des atmosphères subtiles et lumineuses, ornées de tapis ethniques et d'objets décoratifs arabes.

Questa affascinante villa, all'epoca una tenuta dove si produceva vino Malvasia, risale al 1700. I lavori di ristrutturazione avevano come obiettivo conservare lo spirito dell'architettura della zona e dare allo stesso tempo un tocco di modernità. Il bianco mette il risalto la purezza delle linee e l'arredamento crea ambienti delicati e luminosi, adornati con tappeti dagli stampati tribali e oggetti decorativi arabi.

Diese attraktive Villa stammt aus dem Jahre 1700 und war ursprünglich ein Weingut, auf dem Malvasiertrauben verarbeitet wurden. Bei der Umgestaltung sollte trotz Modernisierung die typische Architektur der Region erhalten bleiben. Die weiße Farbe unterstreicht die Klarheit der Linien; die Dekoration lässt geschmackvolle, helle Räume entstehen, die mit Teppichen mit Ethno-Motiven und mit dekorativen Objekten arabischer Herkunft ausgestattet sind.

Deze aantrekkelijke villa dateert van 1700 en was oorspronkelijk een boerderij waar malvezijwijn werd gemaakt. De verbouwing had als doelstelling om de geest van de architectuur van de streek in stand te houden en om die tegelijkertijd in een modern jasje te steken. De kleur wit onderstreept de puurheid van de lijnen en met de inrichting worden delicate en lichte entourages gecreëerd, versierd met vloerkleden met tribale motieven en Arabische snuisterijen.

Esta atractiva villa data de 1700 y era originalmente una finca agrícola donde se fabricaba vino de malvasía. La rehabilitación tenía el objetivo de conservar el espíritu de la arquitectura de la zona y aportar, al mismo tiempo, un matiz moderno. El color blanco realza la pureza de las líneas y la decoración crea ambientes delicados y luminosos, adornados con alfombras de motivos tribales y objetos de decoración árabes.

CHESTERFIELD

Alan Liberman // © Pep Escoda

African sculptures and decorative objects of ethnic influence complement the contemporary architectural design. The result is a space full of contrasts where modernity and tradition are combined with sobriety and comfort.

Sculptures africaines et objets ethniques parachèvent le concept architectural contemporain. Il en résulte un espace rempli de contrastes où le moderne et le classique se mêle avec sobriété et fonctionnalité.

Sculture africane ed oggetti etnici completano lo stile architettonico di natura contemporanea. Il risultato è uno spazio pieno di contrasti dove il moderno e il tradizionale si abbinano con sobrietà e comodità.

Afrikanische Skulpturen und ethnische Objekte ergänzen die architektonische Gestaltung mit zeitgenössischem Charakter. Das Ergebnis sind Räumlichkeiten voller Kontraste, in denen moderne und traditionelle Elemente schlicht und bequem miteinander kombiniert wurden.

Afrikaanse beelden en etnische voorwerpen maken dit bouwproject met een eigentijds karakter compleet. Het resultaat is een ruimte vol met contrast, waarin het moderne en het traditionele op sobere en comfortabele wijze worden gecombineerd.

Esculturas africanas y objetos étnicos complementan el diseño arquitectónico de carácter contemporáneo. El resultado es un espacio lleno de contrastes en el que lo moderno y lo tradicional se combina con sobriedad y comodidad.

CHESTERFIELD
HOTEL

FUCHUN RESORT

Jean-Michel Gathy/Denniston International Group for Fuchun Resort // www.fuchunresort.com // © Fuchun Resort

The elegante of the Chinese ambience of this hotel is given by the use of earthy colors extracted fro the tranquil nature in combination with Chinese classic furniture. The The Quadrangle space style is extracted from the essence of tradicional Jiangnan villages and styled with the contemporary minimalist architectural designs.

Die Eleganz des chinesischen Ambientes in diesem Hotel rührt von den verwendeten natürlichen Erdfarben her, die zusammen mit klassischen chinesischen Möbeln eine harmonische Verbindung eingehen. Der viereckige Hof-Bereich kombiniert das Wesen der traditionellen Dörfer aus dem Jiangnan-Gebiet mit einem modernen Baustil, der vom Minimalismus geprägt ist.

L'atmosphère chinoise, élégante de cet hôtel résulte de l'utilisation de tons ocre inspirés de la nature tranquille et associés à un mobilier chinois classique. L'espace cour s'inspire à la fois de l'essence des villages traditionnels de Jiangnan et des designs contemporains minimalistes.

De elegantie van de Chinese ambiance van dit hotel wordt ingegeven door het gebruik van aardekleuren, afkomstig uit de rustige natuur, in combinatie met Chinese klassieke meubels. De stijl, met de vierhoekige binnenplaatsen, is geïnspireerd op de essentie van traditionele Jiangnan dorpen en is vormgegeven in de stijl van de eigentijdse minimalistische architectuur.

L'elegante atmosfera cinese di questo hotel è data dall'uso di toni naturali color terra combinati con i tipici arredi cinesi. Il modello con spazio quadrangolare riprende l'essenza dei tradizionali villaggi Jiangnan e viene rivisitato con un approccio architettonico minimalista e contemporaneo.

La elegante ambientación china de este hotel se consigue mediante el uso de colores terrosos y naturales que inspiran tranquilidad, aquí combinados con mobiliario chino clásico. El estilo del espacio denominado The Quadrangle toma su esencia de las poblaciones tradicionales de Jiangnan y la conjuga con diseños arquitectónicos minimalistas contemporáneos.

EARTH SPA

DWP – Design Worldwide Partnership // www.dwp.com // © DWP, Evason Hideway

What at first resembles a village in the middle of the rainforest is actually a spa, compriing nine buildings in a circle, which symbolizes the center's underlying holistic philosophy. Their oval shape aims to offset the erosion caused by copious amounts of rain during the monsoon season. The cabins are made with a kind of mud–the result of mixing rice husks, straw, and recycled materials.

À première vue, il pourrait s'agir d'un petit village au milieu de la jungle. Pourtant, il s'agit d'un spa composé de neuf constructions aménagées en cercle, qui se fondent dans le milieu naturel grâce à leur forme et conception. Leur forme voûtée cherche à compenser l'érosion provoquée par les pluies diluviennes de la période des moussons. Les cases sont réalisées à partir d'une matière argileuse issue d'un mélange d'enveloppes de grains de riz, de paille et de matériaux recyclés.

A prima vista sembra un piccolo borgo nel cuore del bosco. Si tratta invece di un centro benessere composto da nove edifici disposti in circolo, che si mimetizzano con l'ambiente circostante sia per la loro forma che per la loro concezione. La forma a cupola mira a contrastare l'erosione causata dalle abbondanti piogge monsoniche. Il materiale con cui sono realizzate le capanne è un'argilla ottenuta dalla miscelazione della parte esterna del chicco di riso, paglia e materiali riciclati.

Auf den ersten Blick wirkt diese Anlage wie ein Dorf inmitten des Urwalds. Es handelt sich jedoch um ein Spa, das neun kreisförmig angeordnete Bauten umfasst, die sowohl aufgrund ihrer Form als auch durch ihre Gestaltung mit der Umgebung verschmelzen. Ihre gewölbte Form soll der Erosion infolge der starken Regenfälle während des Monsuns entgegenwirken. Die Hütten bestehen aus Lehmziegeln, die mit einer Mischung aus Reisschalen, Stroh und recycelten Materialien hergestellt wurden.

Op het eerste gezicht lijkt het een dorp midden in het woud. Het gaat echter om een spa, bestaande uit negen bouwwerken die in een cirkel zijn aangelegd en die zich camoufleren in de omgeving, zowel vanwege hun vorm als conceptie. Door middel van de gewelfde vorm is getracht om te erosie door de overvloedige regenval in de moessontijd tegen te gaan. Het materiaal waarvan de hutten zijn gemaakt is een soort klei dat het resultaat is van een mengeling van rijstschillen, stro en gerecyclede materialen.

A simple vista parece una aldea en medio de la selva. Se trata, sin embargo, de un *spa* compuesto por nueve construcciones dispuestas en círculo, que se mimetizan con el entorno tanto por su forma como por su concepción. Su forma abovedada busca contrarrestar la erosión causada por la copiosa lluvia de la época de los monzones. El material con el que están hechas las cabañas es una arcilla que resulta de la mezcla de cáscara de arroz, paja y materiales reciclados.

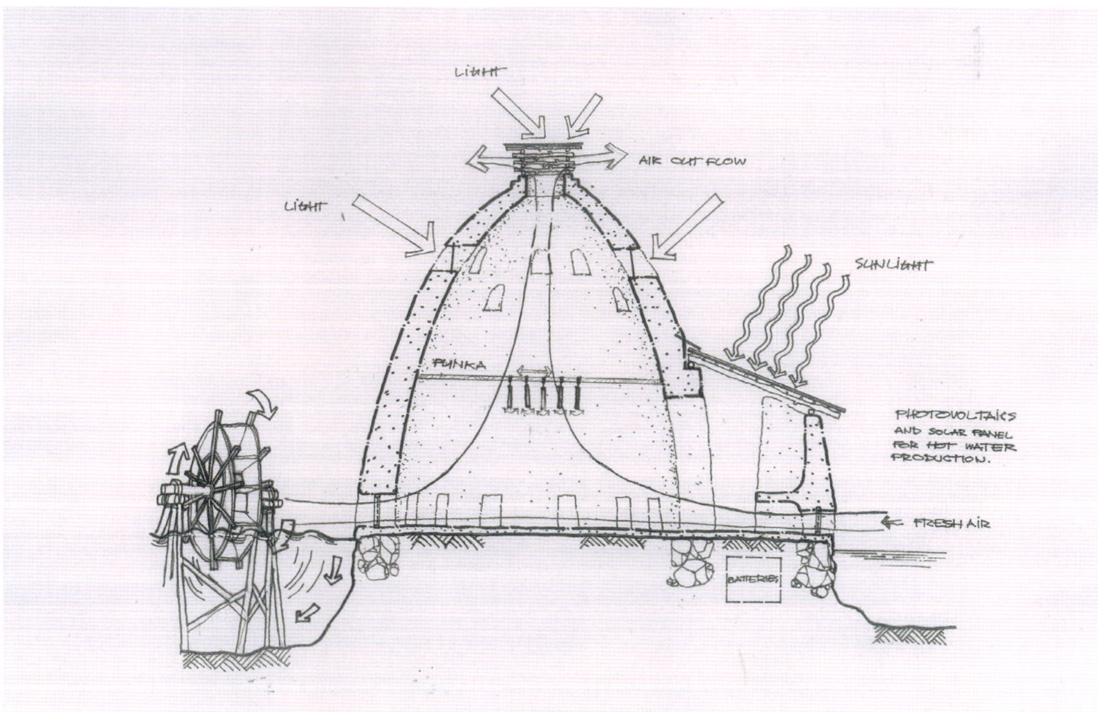

Building concept

BAMBOO GARDEN HOTEL

Bamboo Garden Hotel // www.bbgh.com.cn // © Minoru Iwasaki

The Bamboo Garden Hotel is a classical Chinese courtyard-style structure. The halls and pavillions in the building are linked by tortuous, long corridors, with a tranquil and elegant surrounding of bamboo groves, rockeries, and fountains. All the rooms were newly decorated with new Chinese traditional furniture of Ming & Qing dynasty.

Le Bamboo Garden Hotel est doté d'une structure classique, aux allures de cour intérieure. Les halls et les pavillons du bâtiment sont reliés par de longs couloirs sinueux habillés de rangées de bambous, de rochers et de fontaines qui leur confèrent une atmosphère tranquille et élégante. Toutes les chambres de l'hôtel ont été redécorées avec du mobilier chinois traditionnel des dynasties Ming et Qing.

Il Bamboo Garden Hotel ha una classica struttura a cortile, tipica della tradizione cinese. Le sale e i padiglioni dell'edificio sono collegati da lunghi e tortuosi corridoi e circondati da un'elegante area verde con bambù, rocce e fontane. Tutte le stanze sono state recentemente ristrutturate con arredi tradizionali cinesi di nuova fattura che riproducono pezzi della dinastia Ming e Qing.

Das Bamboo Garden Hotel hat einen klassischen chinesischen Grundriss mit Innenhof. Die Hallen und Pavillons des Gebäudes sind durch lange gewundene Flure miteinander verbunden und von einem ruhigen und eleganten Ambiente mit Bambushainen, Steingärten und Brunnen umgeben. Alle Zimmer wurden mit traditionellen chinesischen Möbeln im Stile der Ming- und Qing-Dynastien eingerichtet.

Het Bamboo Garden Hotel heeft de structuur van een klassieke Chinese binnenplaats. De gangen en paviljoens in het gebouw zijn onderling verbonden door lange, kronkelige gangen, in een rustige en elegante omgeving van bamboebossen, rotstuinen en fonteinen. Alle kamers zijn recentelijk ingericht met nieuw traditioneel Chinees meubilair uit de Ming- en Qing-dynastie.

El Bamboo Garden Hotel es una estructura con patio al estilo clásico de China. Los vestíbulos y pabellones del edificio están unidos por largos y sinuosos pasillos y circundados por un apacible y elegante bosquecillo de bambú, jardín de rocalla y fuentes. Todas las habitaciones se han renovado con mobiliario tradicional chino de las dinastías Ming y Qing.

水上清風移鶴影

CHA JIAFU

Jian Fu // © Minoru Iwasaki

The interior of this teahouse located in Beijing clearly reflects a traditional Chinese style. The paintings with Chinese motifs and letters, the wooden furniture, screens and paper lamps all stand out in this rather austere design. Splashes of color are exclusively reserved for the sofas, upholstered in purple and maroon fabrics.

L'intérieur de cette maison de thé située à Pékin est clairement en ligne avec le style chinois traditionnel. Dans un design relativement austère se distinguent quelques cadres aux motifs et caractères chinois, des meubles en bois, des paravents et des lampes en papier. Les touches de couleur sont réservées aux canapés, recouverts de tissus pourpres et bordeaux.

L'interno di questa casa da tè a Pechino risponde chiaramente alle linee dello stile tradizionale cinese. In un design piuttosto austero si impongono quadri con motivi e lettere cinesi, mobili in legno, paraventi e lampadari di carta. I tocchi di colore sono riservati unicamente ai divani, tappezzati con tessuti porpora e granata.

Das Innere dieses Teehauses in Peking ist eindeutig im traditionellen chinesischen Stil gehalten. Inmitten der recht schmucklosen Gestaltung stechen die Bilder mit chinesischen Motiven und Schriftzeichen, die Holzmöbel, die Paravents und die Lampen mit Papierschirmen hervor. Die einzigen Farbtupfer sind die mit purpurfarbenen und granatroten Stoffen bezogenen Sofas.

Het interieur van dit theehuis, gelegen in Beijing, beantwoordt duidelijk aan de lijnen van de traditionele Chinese stijl. Van het vrij sobere ontwerp vallen de schilderijen met Chinese motieven en letters, de houten meubels, kamerschermen en papieren lampen op. De kleurige details zijn uitsluitend gereserveerd voor de sofa's, die met paarse en granaatkleurige stoffen zijn bekleed.

El interior de esta casa de té situada en Pekín responde claramente a las líneas del estilo tradicional chino. En un diseño bastante austero destacan los cuadros con motivos y letras chinas, los muebles de madera, los biombos y las lámparas de papel. Los toques de color se reservan únicamente a los sofás, tapizados en telas púrpura y granate.

雲海

TOUCH

Stephane Dupoux // www.dupouxdesign.com // © Pep Escoda

The Caribbean context that Miami Beach provides inspires the decorating: lively shapes, thrills of nature and exuberant elegance. Stephane Dupoux designed the club with upbeat sophistication and theatrical lighting and both aspects combines fun and elegance.

L'ambiance des Caraïbes de Miami Beach se retrouve dans la décoration : formes ondoyantes, exaltation de la nature et élégance dans l'exubérance. Stéphane Dupoux a réalisé pour le club un design qui allie raffinement extrême et éclairage théâtral e ces deux aspects créent amusement et élégance.

Il contesto caraibico di Miami Beach ha ispirato la decorazione: forme affilate, esaltazione della naturalezza e eleganza nell'esuberanza di questo bar. Stephane Dupoux ha dotato il locale di un gusto ludico ma sofisticato e di un'illuminazione teatrale e entrambi gli aspetti contribuiscono coniugan divertimento e stile.

Das Karibik-Element von Miami Beach diente als Inspiration bei der Einrichtung: lebendige Formen, Naturschönheiten und überwältigende Eleganz. Stephane Dupoux hat den Club mit Pep und Raffinesse entworfen und eine Theaterbeleuchtung vorgesehen. Das Ergebnis ist eine gut durchdachte Szenerie, die Spaß und Eleganz vereint.

De inrichting is geïnspireerd op de Caribische context van Miami Beach: scherpe vormen, verheerlijking van de natuur en elegantie in de weelderigheid. Stephane Dupoux heeft het plaatselijke karakter voorzien van een ludiek raffinement en theatrale verlichting en beide aspecten komen samen in amusement en elegantie.

El contexto caribeño de Miami Beach inspira la decoración: formas afiladas, exaltación de la naturaleza y elegancia en la exuberancia. Stephane Dupoux ha dotado al local de una lúdica sofisticación e iluminación teatral y ambos aspectos transmiten diversión y elegancia.

BUCHANAN'S

CAFÉ **SAMBAL**

Café Sambal // cho@cafesambal.com // © Minoru Iwasaki

The charm of the *hutong* interior and antique furnishings mixed with some modern fixtures and art Works, gives Café Sambal the air of eccentricty and sophistication for which it is renowed. The softly lit interior allows for a confortable and relaxed dining experience, ideal for romantic occasions.

Le charme de l'intérieur *hutong* et le mobilier ancien, associés à quelques installations et œuvres d'art modernes, confèrent au Café Sambal l'excentricité et la sophistication recherchées. L'éclairage tamisé de cet intérieur est propice à des dîners agréables et relaxants ; il est idéal pour toute occasion romantique.

Il fascino degli interni *hutong* e degli arredi antichi uniti a qualche finitura e opera d'arte moderna, trasmette al Café Sambal l'eccentricità e la sofisticatezza per cui è noto. Gli ambienti interni, caratterizzati da luci leggere e soffuse, consentono di cenare in modo comodo e rilassato e rappresentano il luogo ideale per una serata romantica.

Der besondere Charme des *Hutong*-Interieurs und der antiken Möbel in Verbindung mit einigen modernen Lampen und Kunstwerken verleiht dem Café Sambal die exzentrische Note und das erlesene Flair, für die es bekannt ist. Die sanft beleuchteten Räume laden zum romantischen Abendessen in einem komfortablen und entspannten Rahmen ein.

De charme van het *hutong* interieur en het antieke meubilair, vermengd met enkele moderne kenmerken en kunstwerken, geeft het Café Sambal de sfeer van excentriciteit en raffinement waarvoor het gerenoveerd is. Het zacht verlichte interieur zorgt voor een aangename en ontspannen eetervaring en is ideaal voor romantische aangelegenheden.

El encanto del interior a lo *hutong* y del mobiliario antiguo combinado con ciertos elementos y obras de arte modernos confieren al Café Sambal su renombrado aire de excentricidad y sofisticación. El interior, tenuemente iluminado, permite cenar relajadamente, en un ambiente ideal para las ocasiones románticas.

PORTOLA VALLEY HOUSE

Bob Peterson/Peterson Architects // www.petersonarchitects.com // © Marion Brenner

When the current owners bought this house they wanted to maintain the Asian character created by the original constructor. The combination of Oriental and Western style was familiar to them after having lived for many years in Japan. Therefore, when architect Bob Peterson was commissioned with the extension of the house he kept the same finishes.

Als die Eigentümer dieses Haus erwarben, wollten sie den asiatischen Charakter, der ihm vom ursprünglichen Besitzer verliehen worden war, beibehalten. Die Kombination aus fernöstlichem und westlichem Stil war ihnen durch einen langjährigen Aufenthalt in Japan bereits vertraut. Daher behielt der Architekt Bob Peterson beim Entwurf des Ausbaus die gleichen Materialien bei, einschließlich des Gipses aus Reisschalen.

Lorsque les propriétaires actuels ont acheté cette maison, ils ont décidé de garder le caractère asiatique imprimé par le constructeur initial. Après avoir vécu plusieurs années au Japon, le mariage du style oriental et occidental leur était familier. Par conséquent, lorsque l'architecte Bob Peterson s'est chargé de l'agrandissement de la maison, il a gardé le même type de finitions.

Toen de huidige eigenaren dit huis kochten, wilden ze het oorspronkelijke Aziatische karakter behouden; zij waren al bekend met de combinatie tussen oriëntaalse en westerse stijl doordat ze jarenlang in Japan hadden gewoond. Daarom hield architect Bob Peterson hetzelfde soort afwerkingen aan, waaronder gipsmortel met geïncrusteerde rijstkorrels.

Quando gli attuali proprietari comprarono questa casa, vollero mantenere il carattere asiatico conferito dal costruttore originale. La combinazione dello stile orientale con l'occidentale risultava loro famigliare dopo aver vissuto molti anni in Giappone. Perciò, quando l'architetto Bob Peterson si fece carico dell'ampliamento della casa, mantenne lo stesso tipo di finiture.

Cuando los actuales propietarios compraron esta casa quisieron mantener el carácter asiático original; la combinación del estilo oriental con el occidental les resultaba familiar tras haber vivido muchos años en Japón. Por eso, el arquitecto Bob Peterson mantuvo el mismo tipo de acabados, incluido el yeso con cáscaras de arroz incrustadas.

CAMP HOWIE GARDEN

Jirachai Rengthong/Bensley Design Studios // www.bensley.com/html/eng // © Bensley Design Studios

The exuberant tropical vegetation generates areas that seem to have come straight from a fairy tale. Purchased in neighbouring countries such as Myanmar, Laos and India, the chests, small altars and wooden, stone and metal statues transmit the aesthetic beauty of their rich cultural heritage; they have been strategically placed in various parts of the garden, beckoning to be discovered.

La végétation exubérante tropicale génère des univers qui semblent surgir de contes de fées, à l'instar de l'espace avec la collection de mortiers au cœur d'une forêt de cocotiers. Provenant de pays voisins comme la Birmanie, le Laos ou l'Inde, les coffres, les petits autels et les figurines en bois, en pierre ou en métal, placés à différents endroits stratégiques du jardins, sont là pour être découverts et transmettre le plaisir esthétique de leur riche héritage culturel.

La lussureggiante vegetazione tropicale crea ambienti che sembrano usciti dalle favole. Provenienti da paesi vicini come la Birmania, il Laos e l'India, i bauletti, i piccoli altari e le figure in legno, pietra e metallo strategicamente inserite in vari punti del giardino, invitano alla loro scoperta e trasmettono il gusto estetico della loro ricca eredità culturale.

In einigen Fällen erzeugt die üppige tropische Vegetation ein märchenhaftes Ambiente. Die Truhen, kleinen Altäre und Figuren aus Holz, Stein und Metall, die strategisch in verschiedenen Bereichen des Gartens angesiedelt sind, laden zu ihrer Entdeckung ein und vermitteln den ästhetischen Genuss ihres reichen kulturellen Vermächtnisses.

De weelderige tropische vegetatie schept sprookjesachtige sferen. De uit buurlanden als Birma, Laos en India aangeschafte hutkoffers, kleine altaars en houten, stenen en metalen figuren zijn strategisch geplaatst in verschillende delen van de tuin en nodigen uit om te worden ontdekt. Ze zijn overdragers van het esthetische genot van de rijke culturele erfenis.

La exuberante vegetación tropical genera ambientes que parecen surgidos de cuentos de hadas. Adquiridos en países vecinos, como Birmania, Laos y la India, los cofres, los pequeños altares y las figuras de madera, piedra y metal estratégicamente enclavadas en diferentes áreas del jardín invitan a ser descubiertos y transmiten el placer estético de su rica herencia cultural.

THE BLACK APARTMENT

The Apartment Creative Agency // www.theapt.com // © Michael Weber

Cindy Gallop (owner): "When night falls, I want to feel like I'm in a bar in Shanghai." The answer arrived with a proposal that called for an apartment with black walls, ceilings and floors. There were no dividing walls except in the two bathrooms; where, naturally, privacy should be maintained. The only separations between the rooms would be established by means of thick and weighted curtains.

Cindy Gallop (propriétaire) : « À la tombée de la nuit, je veux me sentir comme dans un bar de Shanghai ». La réponse est arrivée sous la forme d'un appartement noir, du sol au plafond en passant par les murs. Les seules séparations entre les pièces seraient établies au moyen de rideaux lourds et épais, noirs également, qui absorberaient les bruits tout en accentuant la sensation d'opulence.

Cindy Gallop (proprietaria): «Di notte mi piacerebbe sentirmi come in un bar di Shanghai». Come risposta, questi ultimi hanno proposto un appartamento con pareti, soffitti e pavimenti neri. Le uniche divisioni previste tra le stanze sono delle spesse e pesanti tende, anch'esse nere, per assorbire il suono e amplificare il senso di sfarzo.

Cindy Gallop (Eigentümerin): „Jeden Tag bei Einbruch der Dunkelheit will ich mich fühlen, als befände ich mich in einer Bar in Shanghai". Die Designer schlugen eine Wohnung vor, deren Wände, Decken und Böden ganz in Schwarz gehalten sind. Es gibt keine Trennwände. Die einzigen Trennelemente bestehen aus schweren Vorhängen.

Cindy Gallop (eigenaar): "Iedere werkdag, als de avond valt, wil ik het gevoel hebben alsof ik in een bar in Shanghai ben". Het voorstel kwam in de vorm van een appartement met helemaal zwarte wanden, plafonds en vloer. Er zouden geen scheidsmuren bestaan; de enige scheidingen tussen de kamers zijn dikke, zware gordijnen.

Cindy Gallop (propietaria): «Cada jornada, cuando caiga la noche, quiero sentir que estoy en un bar de Shanghai». La propuesta llegó en forma de un apartamento de paredes, techos y suelo completamente negros. No existen paredes divisorias, las únicas separaciones entre los ambientes se establecen mediante gruesas y pesadas cortinas.

God is not
he only one
watching
GALLOP
Paul Richard
80"x48"
mixed media

Paul Richard
80x48

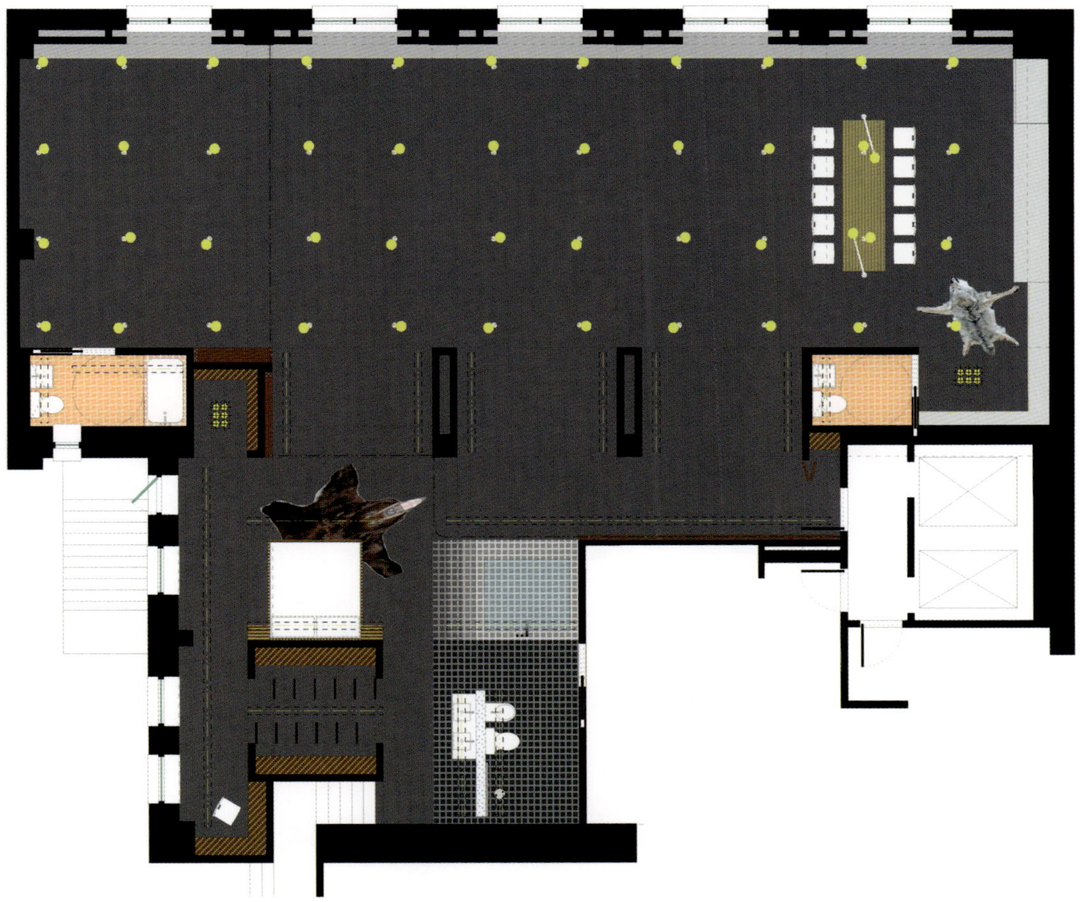

Floor plan

SETTHASIRI PRACHACHUEN

Asian Motifs // www.asianmotifs.com // © Asian Motifs

This residential complex situated in the center of Bangkok is an example of the exotic charm of the Asian culture combined with contemporary architecture. The rattan furniture combines perfectly with the lacquered white tables and chairs, creating a modern interpretation of traditional Chinese design.

Ce complexe résidentiel, situé au centre de la ville de Bangkok, est un exemple du charme exotique de la culture asiatique marié à l'architecture contemporaine. Le mobilier en rotin se marie à merveille aux tables et sièges en blanc laqué, créant une interprétation moderne du design traditionnel chinois.

Questo complesso residenziale situato nel centro della città di Bangkok è un esempio del fascino esotico della cultura asiatica combinato con l'architettura contemporanea. Gli arredi di rattan Si combinano perfettamente con i tavoli e le sedie laccati di bianco, creando un'interpretazione moderna del design tradizionale cinese.

Dieser Wohnkomplex im Zentrum Bangkoks – eine Mischung aus exotisch-asiatischem Flair und moderner Architektur – ist eine Oase, die für das moderne Leben geschaffen wurde. Aufgrund ihres natürlichen Charakters lassen sich die Rattanmöbel leicht mit den weiß lackierten Tischen und Stühlen kombinieren – eine moderne Interpretation des traditionellen chinesischen Designs.

Als ware het een oasis die voor het moderne leven is bedacht, is dit wooncomplex, gelegen in het centrum van de stad Bangkok, een voorbeeld van de exotische charme van de Aziatische cultuur in combinatie met een eigentijdse architectuur. Het rotan meubilair combineert perfect met de witgelakte tafels en stoelen, waardoor het traditionele Chinese ontwerp een moderne interpretatie krijgt.

Como si fuera un oasis pensado para la vida moderna, este complejo residencial situado en el centro de la ciudad de Bangkok es un ejemplo del encanto exótico de la cultura asiática combinado con la arquitectura contemporánea. El mobiliario de ratán armoniza perfectamente con las mesas y sillas lacadas en blanco, creando una interpretación moderna del diseño chino tradicional.

THROUGH THE LENS
NATIONAL GEOGRAPHIC

LOTUS HOUSE

Kengo Kuma & Associates // www.kkaa.co.jp // © Daici Ano

The flower that rises above water is one of the oldest symbols of all cultures. In Asia the lotus, that serves as a throne for Buddha or the Buddhas, indicates a divine birth. The garden has been designed as a link between the riverbank and the building, within which the floral motif is repeated at the foot of a large statue of Buddha.

Dans toutes les cultures, la fleur qui émerge au-dessus de l'eau est un des plus anciens symboles. Chez les asiatiques, le lotus, qui sert de trône pour Bouddha ou les Bouddhas, est le signe d'une naissance divine. Le jardin est ainsi planté comme un lien entre la rivière et l'édifice, à l'intérieur duquel le motif floral se répète sur le socle d'une grande statue de Bouddha.

Il fiore che si erge sull'acqua è uno dei più antichi simboli di tutte le culture. In quella asiatica, il loto che funge da trono per Budda o i Budda, indica una nascita divina. Il giardino è stato concepito come un vincolo tra la riva e l'edificio, in cui il motivo floreale si ripete nel seggio di una grande statua del Budda.

In der asiatischen Kultur dient die Lotosblume – eines der ältesten Symbole – dem Buddha (oder den Buddhas) als Thron und weist auf eine göttliche Geburt hin. Auf diese Weise bildet der Garten eine Grenzfläche zwischen dem Fluss und dem Gebäude, in dem sich das Blumenmotiv auf dem Sockel einer großen Buddha-Statue wiederholt.

De bloem die in het water drijft is een van de oudste symbolen van alle culturen. In de Aziatische cultuur duidt de lotusbloem, die dienst doet als troon voor Boeddha of de Boeddha's, een goddelijke geboorte aan. De tuin is ontworpen als een verbintenis tussen de oever en het gebouw, waarbinnen het bloemenmotief terugkomt in de zitting van een groot Boeddhabeeld.

La flor que flota en el agua es uno de los más antiguos símbolos de todas las culturas. En la asiática, el loto, que sirve como trono para Buda o los Budas, indica un nacimiento divino. El jardín ha sido concebido como un vínculo entre la ribera y el edificio, dentro del cual el motivo floral se repite en el asiento de una gran estatua de Buda.

BAAN SANSIRI SUKHUMVIT

Asian Motifs // www.asianmotifs.com // © Asian Motifs

The interior design is composed of pieces finished in dark tones that contrast with the luminosity of the rooms. A balanced combination of antiques and contemporary furnishings achieves an elegant space of oriental inspiration.

Le design intérieur est composé de pièces aux finitions de couleurs foncées qui contrastent avec la luminosité des pièces. Une alliance équilibrée d'antiquités et de mobilier contemporain permet de créer une ambiance élégante d'inspiration orientale.

Il design degli interni è formato da pezzi dalle finiture scure, che contrastano con la luminosità delle stanze. Attraverso un'equilibrata combinazione d'antichità e arredi contemporanei, è stato possibile creare un ambiente elegante d'ispirazione orientale.

Das Design im Inneren besteht aus dunklen Möbeln, die im Kontrast zur Helligkeit der Räume stehen. Durch die ausgewogene Kombination aus Antiquitäten und modernen Möbeln wurde ein elegantes und zugleich orientalisch anmutendes Ambiente geschaffen.

Het interieurontwerp bestaat uit onderdelen met afwerkingen in donkere tinten, die contrasteren met de lichtheid van de vertrekken. Door middel van een evenwichtige combinatie van antiek en eigentijds meubilair is men erin geslaagd om een elegante, oosters geïnspireerde sfeer te creëren.

El diseño interior se compone de piezas con acabados de tonos oscuros que contrastan con la luminosidad de las estancias. A través de una equilibrada combinación de antigüedades y mobiliario contemporáneo se ha logrado crear un ambiente elegante de inspiración oriental.

HUANG TING RESTAURANT IN THE PENINSULA PALACE HOTEL

Chhada Siembieda and Associates Ltd. // © Peninsula Palace Beijing

Based on a tradicional nobleman's house, Huang Ting succeeds in recreating a genuine *hutong* feel, with the heavy studded wooden front door, aged pine flooring and carved timber screens recycled from demolition sites in Shangxi Province in Beijing, as old courtyards are replaced by modern buildings.

Sur la base d'une maison d'aristocrate traditionnelle, Huang Ting parvient à recréer une atmosphère *hutong* authentique : une porte d'entrée cloutée en bois massif, un plancher en bois de pin vieilli et des panneaux en bois sculpté récupérés sur des sites de démolition dans la province de Shanxi à Pékin où les vieilles cours sont remplacées par des immeubles contemporains.

Il Huang Ting, che si erge sulla casa tradizionale di un nobile, riesce a ricreare un'atmosfera *hutong* autentica con la pesante e robusta porta di ingresso in legno, i pavimenti di pino stagionato e le protezioni in legno lavorato recuperate dalle discariche nella provincia di Shangxi a Pechino, dato che le antiche case con cortile vengono sostituite da edifici moderni.

Das im Herzen von Peking gelegene Restaurant Huang Ting, das vom traditionellen Zuhause eines Adligen inspiriert wurde, erweckt eine echte *Hutong*-Atmosphäre – hier wurden eine mit Nieten beschlagene Eingangstür aus Holz, ein Bodenbelag aus gealtertem Kiefernholz und geschnitzte Holzpaneele verarbeitet, die aus Abrisshäusern in der Provinz Shanxi gerettet werden konnten, wo moderne Bauten die althergebrachten Wohnhöfe mehr und mehr verdrängen.

Bij de bouw van Huang Ting, gebaseerd op een traditioneel herenhuis, is men erin geslaagd om het authentieke *hutong* gevoel weer op te roepen, met de zware houten voordeur, oud grenenhouten vloeren en kamerschermen gerecycled uit sloopterreinen in de provincie Shangxi in Beijing, toen oude patio's werden vervangen door moderne gebouwen.

Al estilo de una casa de la aristocracia tradicional, el Huang Ting logra recrear un auténtico ambiente de *hutong*, merced a su gruesa puerta frontal de madera tachonada, sus suelos de pino envejecido y sus biombos de madera tallada, reciclados de obras de demolición de la provincia pekinesa de Shangxi, donde los patios de antaño están siendo reemplazados por edificios modernos.

GARDEN **IN BERLIN-MARZAHN**

Shunmyo Masuno/Japan Landscape Consultants // www.kenkohji.jp // © Japan Landscape Consultants

The main elements of the front gardens are the pond and creek. In the southeast area of the garden a cascade of stones symbolizes Germany's origins. The pavilion, called Nyosuitei, consists of an open *sukiyaki* style building that offers a space from where one can contemplate the garden.

Les principaux éléments du jardins sont le bassin et la cascade. Dans la zone sud-est du jardin, une cascade de pierres symbolise l'origine de l'Allemagne. Le pavillon, appelé Nyosuitei, est une construction ouverte du style *sukiyaki*, offrant un espace d'où il est possible de contempler le jardin.

Gli elementi principali dei giardini sono il laghetto e il torrente. Nella zona sud-est del giardino, una cascata di pietre simbolizza l'origine della Germania. Il padiglione, chiamato Nyosuitei, è un'edificazione aperta in stile *sukiyaki*, che offre uno spazio da cui contemplare il giardino.

Die Hauptelemente des vorderen Gartens sind der Teich und der Wasserlauf. Ein Steinwasserfall im südöstlichen Teil des Gartens symbolisiert die Quelle, den Ursprung der Geschichte Deutschlands. Der Nyosuitei genannte Pavillon besteht aus einem offenen Gebäude im *Sukiyaki*-Stil, aus dessen Inneren man den Garten betrachten.

De belangrijkste elementen van de tuinen aan de voorzijde zijn de vijver en het beekje. In het zuidoostelijke gedeelte van de tuin symboliseert een waterval met stenen de oorsprong van Duitsland. Het paviljoen, genaamd Nyosuitei, bestaat uit een open gebouw in *sukiyaki*-stijl die toegang biedt naar een ruimte van waaruit men de tuin kan bekijken en het bewustzijn wordt aangescherpt.

Los principales elementos de los jardines frontales son el estanque y el riachuelo. En la zona sudeste del jardín, una cascada de piedras simboliza el origen de Alemania. El pabellón, llamado Nyosuitei, consiste en una edificación abierta al estilo *sukiyaki*, que ofrece un espacio desde el cual contemplar el jardín.

融合如水以成和

ELENA STANIC APARTMENT

Elena Stanic (Owner) // © Bisou Foto

This apartment revolves around a single space which includes three different areas: the kitchen, the living room and the studio. Contemporary furniture mixes with ethnic style cushions and tables. The bedroom, situated in a separate room, has a space for a bathtub decorated with candles. The plants lend an exotic touch to the apartment.

Cette demeure dispose d'un seul espace ouvert qui s'articule autour de trois zones différenciées : la cuisine, le salon et le studio. Le mobilier se mêle à des coussins et tables de style ethnique. La chambre à coucher, située dans une pièce à part, dispose d'un espace agrémenté d'une baignoire décorée de bougies. Les plantes contribuent à l'exotisme de l'ensemble.

Questo attico è composto da un solo spazio aperto suddiviso in tre zone distinte: la cucina, il soggiorno e lo studio. La mobilia in stile contemporaneo si combina con i cuscini e i tavoli in stile etnico. Nella camera da letto, situata in un vano indipendente, è da notare la vasca da bagno decorata con candele. Le piante contribuiscono a dare un tocco esotico all'insieme.

Die Dachgeschosswohnung ist ein großer offener Raum, in dem drei unterschiedliche Wohnbereiche untergebracht sind: Küche, Wohnzimmer und Atelier. Zeitgenössische Möbel werden mit Kissen und Tischen im Ethno-Stil kombiniert. In einem separaten Raum befindet sich das Schlafzimmer, in einer Ecke des Raumes steht eine mit Kerzen verzierte Badewanne. Zahlreiche Pflanzen tragen zur Exotik des Gesamtbildes bei.

Deze woning heeft slechts een open ruimte, waarin zich drie verschillende zones onderscheiden: de keuken, zitkamer en werkruimte. Het eigentijdse meubilair is gecombineerd met kussens en tafels in etnische stijl. In de slaapkamer staat een met kaarsen gedecoreerd bad. De planten dragen bij aan het exotische karakter van het geheel.

Esta vivienda dispone de un solo espacio abierto en el que se distribuyen tres áreas diferenciadas: la cocina, la sala de estar y el estudio. El mobiliario contemporáneo se mezcla con los cojines y las mesas de estilo étnico. El dormitorio cuenta con un espacio dotado de una bañera decorada con velas. Las plantas contribuyen al exotismo del conjunto.

SUMMER WORKSHOPS
mamori
artlab

Pando